WALL OF SHAME

HUMANITY
Patrick Bonneville Society

WALL OF SHAME

THE 100 GREATEST
FAILURES OF HUMANITY

**DESIGNED BY
PATRICK BONNEVILLE**

This book is dedicated to a special 13-year-old girl, Aisha. According to Amnesty International, on October 27th 2007, the young Aisha Ibrahim Duhulow was stoned to death by a group of 50 men in the southern port of Kismayu. Somalia. The event happended in a stadium in front of 1,000 spectators who came to applaud this execution. She had been accused of adultery in breach of Islamic law.

Aisha, nobody deserves what happened to you. I am sorry none of us came to your rescue. We failed you.

Patrick Bonneville

Published by
PATRICK BONNEVILLE SOCIETY
310 Parmenter, Sutton, Quebec
J0E 2K0 Canada
www.patrickbonneville.ca

Writer: Kim Murray
Research: Kim Murray, Patrick Bonneville
Editor: Shannon Partridge
Proofreading: Kelli Ann Ferrigan
Designer: Patrick Bonneville
Consultant designer: Philippe Hemono

Cover design: Patrick Bonneville
Back cover text: Shannon Partridge
Cover picture: Aron Brand/Shutterstock
Half title page: Lane Erickson/Dreamstime.com
Full title page: Otnaydur/Dreamstime.com

Printed and bound in Hong Kong

ISBN 978-1-926654-04-1

Legal deposit - Bibliothèques et Archives
nationales du Québec, 2010

Legal deposit - Library and Archives Canada,
2010

Series created by Patrick Bonneville

Produced with the support of Quebec Refund-
able Tax Credit for Book Production Services and
Sodexport program.

SODEC
Québec

The publisher offers special thanks to
Kim Murray, Shannon Partridge, Kelli
Ann Ferrigan, Gina Garza, Lori Baird,
Isabelle Paradis and Philippe Hemono.
The publisher also thanks Céline
Laprise, Caroline Leclerc and Louis
Dubé from the SODEC. *Merci à tous.*

"A genocide begins with the killing of one man – not for what he has done, but because of who he is. A campaign of 'ethnic cleansing' begins with one neighbour turning on another. Poverty begins when even one child is denied his or her fundamental right to education. What begins with the failure to uphold the dignity of one life, all too often ends with a calamity for entire nations."
—Kofi Annan

C O N T E N T S

Photo credit: Angela Campanelli

This book is an important reminder of humanity's faults and frailties from the recent past. History tends to repeat itself, so it is important we learn from it. This is especially important as we humans grow in numbers—more than ever before we must interact, work together, in the same "global village." We are all bound together, not just by simple virtue of our humanity, but by our economies.

In *Wall of Shame,* we have created a list of events from the dark side of humanity. They are the 100 events that we think everybody should know about. They are 100 situations that cannot be repeated or that need to change. They are 100 lessons for humanity.

The world we have built is often a very cruel one. Sadly, the twentieth century and the first years of the twenty-first only confirm this. Terrible events created by groups of people have had devastating effects on the lives of others, often innocent lives.

This has happened all over the Earth, but we in the West have a role in this too: our fast-paced world, where more is always better, causes the whole planet to suffer in the name of consumer goods and gasoline. Wars are started around the world to support the arms industry. They are also started for control of the resources we need to maintain our safe and easy lifestyles. Worst of all, perhaps, is that the environment is in jeopardy; if it goes, we go.

We did not want to go too far back in time in naming the worst incidents of violence and repression that have taken place around the world. We wanted to find events that were close to us, with only a few generations separating the past from the present. We decided to only go as far back as World War II, which was the largest-scale destructive event in the history of humanity. That said, we have made a handful of exceptions for events that happened just before the whole world was drawn into war's territory. They were significant events that marked the course of our recent history. Other events that we list were yesterday's headlines. And, unfortunately, others are happening right now, as you read this.

Patrick Bonneville

The Ranking Process

Many publishing folk and friends have asked me about the top-100 format of the HUMANITY books. Why did we choose a subjective ranking process? Well, here is my most honest answer: we want to make a statement. By listing these events in a preferential order, we can put emphasis on the ones we think are worth the most attention.

Ranking also creates debate. We want people to think more about these tragic events and situations and talk about them. Ranking leads us to challenge and defend what is important to us and to humanity. Ranking the Wall of Shame challenges our humanitarian values, deep down inside.

On the other hand, our ranking is certainly not absolute truth. We acknowledge our Western bias. We acknowledge the limitations of our research. We also acknowledge that one life lost is a tragedy and that millions of lives lost is a million tragedies. A human life, anywhere—even in a faraway place—is not merely a statistic.

Suffering is suffering, yes, but some events are just too dark, have affected too many people, and have taken too many lives: they have to be ranked first. On the other hand, some others, less known and less covered by the media, are also worth a place in this book. There were plenty of tragedies in the past few decades, and plenty of injustices, but we have chosen 100 of them.

We hope you will agree with some of these choices.

We chose to apply five criteria in ranking the Wall of Shame:

Human Rights
To what extent have universal human rights been violated?

Violence
What was the degree of violence used?

World reach
How many countries were affected by the situation or by the conflict?

Inevitability
Could the conflict or the problem been avoided?

Destruction
How many people died or were injured? How badly damaged were infrastructure, environment, and private property?

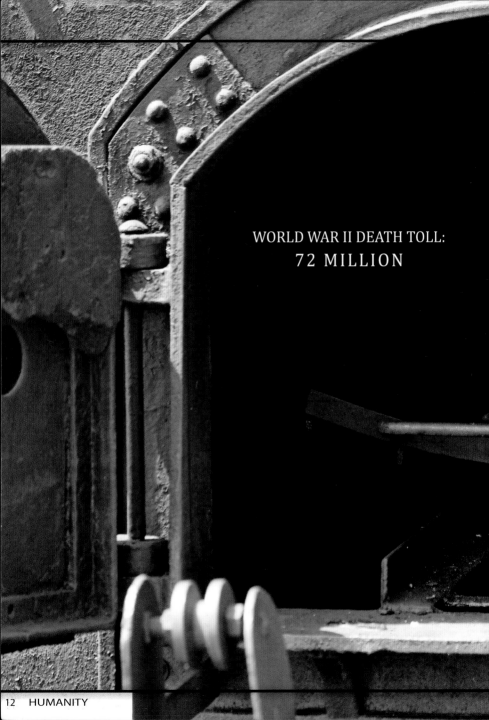

WORLD WAR II DEATH TOLL:
72 MILLION

Patrick Bonneville: The world was never uglier than during World War II. This was humanity at its worst. Genocides, mass killings, families torn apart, the suffering of children, segregation, weapons of mass destruction, nuclear armament, slavery, forced labor, rape, scientific experiments on humans. The list is too long. It seemed like every part of the world was putting its resources and efforts into one common goal: war. Humanity will not survive a World War III; the Earth might not either.

World War II officially lasted six years, from September 1, 1939 to September 2, 1945. Total deaths: 72 million. Civilian deaths: 47 million, including 20 million from war-related disease and famine.

World War I left many European countries bitter. In Germany, frustration was ripe after the Treaty of Versailles, in which considerable amounts of land had been taken away and attributed to other nations. Under the Nazi regime, Germany began to develop plans to reclaim what it considered its rightful lands. These territories included the Polish Corridor, Danzig, the Memel Territory, the Province of Posen, and the province of Alsace-Lorraine. It was also eager to regain authority over Saarland and the Rhineland. Bitterness was strong in Hungary as well, and that country hoped to recover its losses by allying with Germany.

Right: Adolf Hitler led the world to World War II.
Opposite page: Auschwitz II-Birkenau. These rails led 1.1 million to their death.

Italy felt neglected after having helped the Allies achieve victory in World War I. Italian Prime Minister Benito Mussolini initiated expansion into other territories, invading Ethiopia in 1935 and Albania in 1939. His goal: to create a new Roman Empire.

Death toll, by country:
- Soviet Union: 23 million
- China: 20 million, mostly civilians
- Germany: 6 million
- Poland: 5.6 million
- Japan: 2.7 million
- India: 1.5 million civilians
- France: 567,600
- United Kingdom: 450,000
- United States: 416,800 soldiers

"As soon as the idea was introduced that all men were equal before God, that world was bound to collapse."
—Adolf Hitler, February 26, 1942

"*The world must know what happened, and never forget.*"
—*General Eisenhower, while visiting Nazi death camps, 1945*

Other events snowballed. Rapid hyper-inflation hampered economic growth throughout parts of Europe, and the USA and Britain were buried in war debt. The Spanish Civil War divided European loyalties in half, while Germany's Adolf Hitler undertook economic and military cooperation with China in 1938 in order to ally against the Soviet Union. The Japanese needed more resources to feed their imperial quest into Asia, and the Second Sino-Japanese war drew in, at different points, Germany, the Soviet Union, and the United States.

These combined political desires and ambitions were a perfect prelude to war. Most agree that World War II started on September 1, 1939 with the invasion of Poland by Germany. It was not long before Poland's western allies gathered in battle. By October 2, the "Allies" were Australia, France (including overseas territories), New Zealand, the UK, Newfoundland, Canada, Nepal, South Africa, and Czechoslovakia. The Soviet Union switched sides after Germany invaded that country. During the course of the war, dozens of countries joined forces with the Allies.

Left: World War II memorial in Volgograd, Russia.
Right: American Cemetery, Margraten, Netherlands.

As Germany and its allies—the "Axis Powers"—continued their various invasions, many more countries joined the war. The Axis Powers were Germany, Japan, Italy (eventually only Northern Italy), Hungary, Romania, Croatia, Slovakia, Bulgaria, and Thailand.

It seemed the whole world was engaged in this formidable war on many fronts, right up until the official surrender of Japan, on September 2, 1945. Germany had surrendered unconditionally on May 8, 1945, a day now celebrated as Victory Day in Europe. The devastating and costly WWII was characterized by an unheard of breadth of geography, violence, and horrible acts previously unknown on that scale. Some of its worst war crimes are described here.

The Holocaust
The Holocaust refers to the genocide of approximately six million European Jews during World War II. It was an organized and cohesive strategy for the extermination of Jews that was implemented by Adolf Hitler's Nazi regime. If the other groups Hitler targeted for extermination are considered—including ethnic Poles, the Romani, Soviet civilians, Soviet prisoners of war, people with disabilities, gay men, and

political and religious opponents—the Nazi's slaughter totals between 11 and 17 million people.

It is known now that Hitler's genocide began several years before the outbreak of WWII. As the Third Reich (Hitler's regime) first expanded into new territories, they murdered Jews and political opponents in mass shootings. Others were driven to concentration camps, and still others were forced into slavery. Many died of disease, and those who weren't, were eventually executed in gas chambers. Every branch of the Nazi regime was involved in the implementation of this program of mass murder.

The Nanking Massacre

In the lead-up to the Asian front of World War II, Japan invaded and captured Nanking, then the capital of the Republic of China. The six weeks following the December 9, 1937 invasion are now known as the Rape of Nanking, or The Nanking Massacre. The Imperial Japanese Army participated in atrocities such as rape, looting, arson, and the execution of prisoners of war and civilians. The invasion came to light at the end of WWII with the international community agreeing that Japan's actions amounted to the severest of war crimes.

One Japanese soldier is reported to have said that on December 13, 1937, more than 50,000 Chinese, including children, were shot dead. Another infamous account tells the story of two

Japanese soldiers holding a killing contest, in which the idea was to kill 100 people using a sword. Over a number of days, this horrific incident unfolded like a sporting event, with updates and scores. Journalist Matsumoto Shigeharu, of the Shanghai office of the Domei News Agency wrote, "The reason that the Yanagawa Corps [the 10th Army] is advancing [to Nanking] as rapidly is due to the tacit consent among the officers and men that they could loot and rape as they wish."

In December 1941, the Japanese military officially adopted *Sankō Sakusen,* or the "burn-to-ashes" strategy that included "kill all, burn all, and loot all." The policy leaves little doubt about the mentality and intention of the army's leaders at the time. Some Japanese historians and government officials maintain today that this event has been grossly exaggerated as Chinese propaganda. It remains a delicate matter in

"Women are being carried off every morning, afternoon and evening. The whole Japanese army seems to be free to go and come as it pleases, and to do whatever it pleases."
—Reverend James M. McCallum, Nanking

Sino-Japanese relations as well as in Japan's relationships with other Asian-Pacific nations such as Korea, Australia, and the Philippines.

Invasion of Poland
During the German and Soviet invasion of Poland from September 1 to October 6, 1939, German aircraft targeted civilian refugees marching on roads in order to dampen Polish morale. Thousands of Polish civilians and POWs were also assassinated. At Operation Tannenburg, nearly 20,000 Poles were shot at public execution sites. The total estimate of death on this front of the war is 150,000 to 200,000 Poles.

The Paradis Massacre
On May 27, 1940, German SS Division Totenkopf lined up and assassinated ninety-seven British soldiers who had barricaded themselves inside a farmhouse. They were discovered by German troops and forced to surrender. Two British soldiers escaped and were recaptured several days later.

Normandy
Following the D-Day landings, during which the Allies disembarked upon the beaches of Northern Normandy, 156 Canadian prisoners of war were executed by 12th SS Panzer Division (the Hitler Youth) in France's Normandy countryside.

The Malmedy Massacre
Near Baugnez, Belgium, German troops killed ninety American prisoners of war on December 17, 1944.

The Lidice Massacre
In a vengeful and brutal act, 192 men over 16 years of age from this village in the Czech Republic were murdered by the German SS on June 10, 1942. The remaining citizens were forced into concentration camps, where many of the women and the majority of the children were subsequently killed. The village was then burned to the ground until all traces of its existence had vanished. Two weeks later, the nearby village of Lezaky was also destroyed and its residents murdered.

Jasenovac
During WWII, thousands of people were murdered at Jasenovac, in occupied Yugoslavia, now the Republic of Croatia. According to the United States Holocaust Memorial Museum, Croat authorities killed an estimated 52,000 Serb residents of the then-called Independent State of Croatia. The numbers of political and religious opponents of the Croat regime who met death at the hands of Croats are shocking. Estimates suggest that between 8,000 and 20,000 Jews, between 8,000 and 15,000 Romani, and between 5,000 and 12,000 ethnic Croats and Muslims died at Jasenovac.

"Germany has concluded a Non-Aggression Pact with Poland... We shall adhere to it unconditionally. We recognize Poland as the home of a great and nationally conscious people."
—Adolf Hitler, May 21, 1935

The Death Marches

During the winter of 1944-45, mostly Jewish prisoners were forcibly transferred from German concentration camps near the war front to camps in-country. The Nazis were feeling the squeeze of approaching Allied forces to the West and Soviet forces to the East. The Nazis, not wanting the full horrors of the concentration camps to be revealed, evacuated them. The prisoners—starving, beaten, sick, and barely clothed—were forced to march tens of kilometers in winter weather. Thousands of concentration camp prisoners were murdered before the marches even began. Many of the Nazi perpetrators were tried later at the Nuremberg trials for crimes against humanity.

The Porajmos

Porajmos, "devouring" in the Romani language, refers to the assassination of Romani people, sometimes known as "gypsies." War crimes against the itinerant Romani are largely ignored in the body of Holocaust information. Although difficult to confirm today, some estimates suggest that anywhere from 220,000 to over 1,500,000 Romani died at the hands of the Nazis.

The Manila Massacre

In this one-month bloodbath at the hands of Japanese forces in Manila, Philippines, at least 100,000 innocent lives were destroyed. Frustrated by the order for withdrawal of Japanese troops by Imperial Army General Tomoyuki Ymashita, 10,000 marines, under Vice Admiral Snaji Iwabuchi, remained behind to literally kill civilians at will. This event marks one of the worst crime scenes of the war. No one was safe; abuses and killings were doled out indiscriminately to women, children, priests, Red Cross personnel, prisoners of war, and hospital patients.

The war crimes and the crimes committed against humanity on all the fronts of World War II are, unfortunately, plentiful, from both sides. All of them would easily fill our Wall of Shame. We hope that the world has learned something from them.

"We saw terrible things: cremated adults shrunk to the size of small children, pieces of arms and legs, dead people, whole families burnt to death, burning people ran to and from, burnt coaches filled with civilian refugees, dead rescuers and soldiers, many (of whom) were calling and looking for their children and families."
—Lothar Metzger, survivor of the Dresden bombing

Human rights	10/10
Violence	10/10
World reach	10/10
Inevitability	6/10
Destruction	10/10
Average score	9.2/10

"*Slavery was abolished 150 years ago, right? While it is true that slavery is illegal almost everywhere on earth, the fact is there are more slaves today than there ever were...*"
—*Robert Alan*

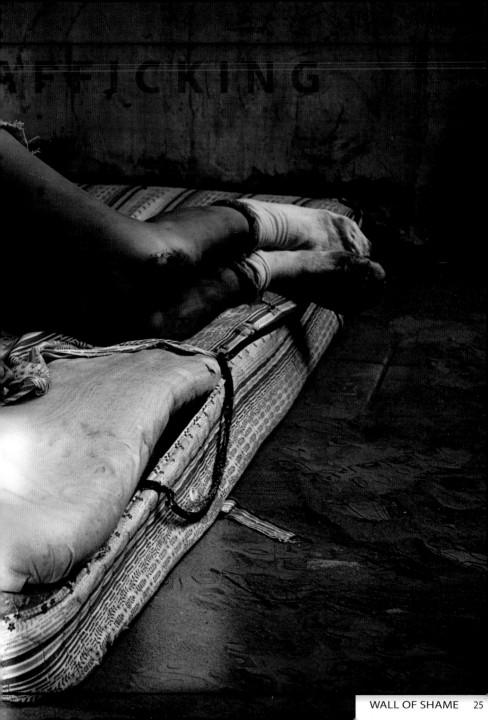

AFFICKING

The face of slavery today is as frightening as it ever was in the days of our ancestors, in the far-away countries we only ever heard about. Today, we wear T-shirts made by virtual slaves. Our children play with the toys they make. Some of our men view the pornography they perform. Human trafficking is what it is called today, but the end result is the same: a displacement from one's home, then forced labor with no end to its terms and no recompense for the worker.

Under the promise of immigration papers, human trafficking brings people from underdeveloped economies to Western cities where they must work off their debt in textile sweatshops. Human trafficking brings prostitutes—women and children, both girls and boys—to be forced to work in prostitution rings or pornography production. And it is a dozen other degrading, hopeless, and disturbing ways humans have found to profit from those who are desperate and unprotected.

Human trafficking is the fastest growing criminal industry in the world. It includes both legal and illegal activities that amount to estimated global revenues of between $5 and $9 billion. According to the United Nations, human trafficking includes organ trafficking, bonded labor, involuntary servitude, domestic servitude and child labor. Its activities are often well-hidden from the public's view.

Above: Children are easy targets.
Right: There are 10,000 women being held in Los Angeles' underground brothels.

Organ Trafficking

Organ trafficking is an organized crime that begins when a recruiter finds a victim. The crime implicates participation at many levels: hospitals or clinics, medical professionals, middlemen and contractors, buyers, banks where they are stored, and possibly other dimensions not yet identified.

In this involuntary trade, the victims' body organs are taken without their knowledge or else removed under false pretences with no compensation. Some people are coerced into giving up an organ or agree to sell it from sheer financial desperation. In this case, they are often cheated out of the monies promised them. Others undergo surgery for another procedure—sometimes for legitimate treatment, other times under completely false pretences—and wake up to find an organ has been removed without their knowledge.

Many of the victims of organ trafficking are migrants, homeless, or illiterate. The most commonly traded or stolen organs include kidneys and the liver, although any organ that can be removed and used on the illegal trade market is vulnerable.

Organ trafficking seems to be on the rise. It is believed that 10 percent of all organ transplants performed around the world are obtained through the black market and organ trafficking.

Bonded Labor

This is the exploitation of a person who believes themselves to be indebted to the perpetrator. It is often called "bonded labor" or "debt bondage." In a typical scenario, the worker falls into this situation by accepting to work in exchange for money loans or for immigration papers. The repayment expected in labor far exceeds the value of the money or service traded. In some cases, and in some countries, the debt is passed from generation to generation, meaning that entire families can be enslaved for decades. According to Anti-Slavery International, there are currently at least 20 million bonded laborers in the world today.

Involuntary Servitude

Victims of involuntary servitude are trapped into work agreements that are enforced by threat of serious physical harm or legal consequences, such as deportation. They often experience physical and verbal abuse and are intimidated into a submission that prevents them from ever receiving information about their actual rights. Victims are often economic migrants or low-skilled laborers trafficked from developing nations to prosperous ones.

Left: Two-thirds of women trafficked for prostitution worldwide come from Eastern Europe.

Domestic Servitude

Similar to involuntary servitude, victims are trapped by coercion into service in private homes. Women, and especially children, are the main targets; they are usually illegal immigrants brought from poorer countries to serve wealthy Western families. At the best of times, domestic work is unregulated because it is removed from the public eye. In many situations of this kind of human trafficking, the victims are subjected to physical, sexual, or emotional abuse.

Child Labor

Perhaps the most recognized from of human trafficking is child labor, in which children are sold or traded into bonded or forced labor. In many countries around the world, children may legally obtain "light" work whose wages their families rely on. Child labor also includes the use of children in armed conflicts, military operations, or military training for future operations. Children are often forced into these situations for their very survival, or for that of their family. Sometimes they are lured into work under the false promise of freedom.

"The Security Council has said that it will consider sanctions against governments and armed groups that refuse to end their use of child soldiers. Instead, it has allowed these crimes against children to continue for years."
—Jo Becker, children's rights advocate at Human Rights Watch

Regardless of the form it takes, human trafficking is slavery. Its victims generally have no means to obtain their own freedom, at least not that they themselves are aware of. They typically have no access to education or medical assistance, and they have no way of communicating with authorities that could help them. The U.S. Department of State estimates that, internationally, there are between 600,000 and 800,000 humans trafficked yearly. If we add those who are trafficked within domestic borders, the number would jump drastically.

The forced labor market costs the world about $20 billion each year; there is a huge economic incentive to end forced labor and to bring about decent living conditions for every human. In 2000, the United Nations introduced the Convention against Transnational Organized Crime, also known as the Palermo Convention. Two specific protocols called for the prevention, suppression, and punishment for the trafficking of persons and a protocol against the smuggling of migrants through all means of transport. The International Labor Organization has launched a program to abolish forced labor, in all its forms, by 2015. They have joined forces with several international organizations in lobbying governments to take measures to combat these kinds of slavery.

Left: Child labor in Pakistan.

It is also essential that the individual consumer be part of this global alliance to end human trafficking, whose victims are producing services and goods that we consume. If we buy a T-shirt, let's consider who picked the cotton and where it was made. Was it made by a slave? A sweatshop worker? A child? Let's be aware of where our products come from and let's support programs that are working to eradicate forced labor.

"Our research shows that there are at least 27 million people in slavery around the world today. And that's real slavery -- people held against their will, under violence or threat of violence, and paid nothing."
—*Jolene Smith, executive director of Free the Slaves*

"We could eradicate slavery. The laws are in place. The multi-nationals, the world trade organizations, the United Nations, they could end slavery, but they're not going to do it until and unless we demand it."
—*Kevin Bales*

Human rights	10/10
Violence	910
World reach	10/10
Inevitability	8/10
Destruction	7.5/10
Average score	8.9/10

"Comrade Stalin, having become Secretary-General, has unlimited authority concentrated in his hands, and I am not sure whether he will always be capable of using that authority with sufficient caution."
—*Excerpt from* Lenin's Testament

Patrick Bonneville: Statues of this man still stand in some places. Some consider him a hero for elevating the Soviet Union to superpower status. Most of the world sees, however, that he was one of the most brutal tyrants of all time. Despite being on the side of the allies during World War II, this man and his regime committed the most unbelievable atrocities against his own people and against humanity. The announcement of the death of Joseph Stalin in 1953 was a relief for people everywhere.

Joseph Stalin was at the helm of the Soviet Union from 1924 until his death in 1953. He rose to power after the death of Vladimir Lenin and went on to squeeze his people and his nation into a tight and terrifying existence. During his reign, Stalin was the General Secretary of the Communist Party of the Soviet Union's Central Committee—abbreviated to Politiburo. While he had full control, he was definitely not popular.

By the 1930s he was already on a killing streak, eliminating those who opposed him. In the 1934 party elections, Stalin received 1,108 negative votes, while his rival, Sergei Kirov, received three. Not long after, on December 1, 1934, Kirov was assassinated. It is widely believed that Stalin ordered the attack, yet Stalin himself quickly called for justice. An assassin was found, tried, and hung. Other aspects of his legacy are worse:

The Great Purge
The Great Purge or the Great Terror saw Stalin attempt to wipe out all opposition. With the Soviet Union trying to recover from the severe famine of 1932-1933, Stalin drafted a campaign to purge his party of all "corruption and treachery." His Great Purge extended to the military and to civilians as well.

Suspects were executed, or, worse, imprisoned in the Gulag labor camps. Archive data shows that Stalin ordered the imprisonment of 1,548,367 citizens, of whom 681,692 were executed in 1937-38—roughly 1,000 murders every day. Countless others died while in the Gulag. Some estimates suggest that the total number of deaths from the Great Purge is over 1.2 million. These statistics do not include the millions of ethnic minorities who were deported.

Mass graves were found at Bykivnia, where an estimated 120,000 - 225,000 corpses were buried. At Kurapaty, an estimated 30,000 to 200,000 bodies were found; at Butovo, over 20,000 were confirmed killed, and at Sandarmokh, over 9,000 bodies were discovered.

Upper left: Joseph Vissarionovich Stalin.
Right: Holodomor memorial in Kiev, Ukraine.

"The death of one man is a tragedy. The death of millions is a statistic."
—*Joseph Stalin*

The Holodomor

Holodomor is the Ukrainian term for "death by starvation." In 1932-33, under direct orders by Stalin, farmers were forced into collective farming; the result was an apparently deliberate, man-made catastrophe. More people died in the Soviet Union from this starvation-by-design than during the whole of World War II. The exact number of deaths due to starvation is unknown, but experts put the figure between 2.6 and 10 million. This was not war; nor was it a natural disaster. It was policy.

Some people contend that the cause of the Holodomor was an unforseen result of policy or of economic problems associated with the rise of Soviet industrialization. There is reason to believe, however, that this event was Stalin's vengeful attack on the Ukrainian people; if so, then the event falls under the legal definition of genocide. In October 2008, the European Parliament declared the Holodomor to be a crime against humanity. Ukraine and nineteen other countries concurred.

As Stalin rode the fear of his people to the summit of power, he built up secret armies and prisons to reshape his nation. His goal was to build an economically strong country that had no room for weakness and defiance. All his opponents had to be silenced. He confiscated farm land from the better-off peasants, who were rounded up, killed, or deported. By 1937, along with the Holodomor, Stalin's regime was responsible for the murder of at least 14.5 million people.

Gulag

Possibly the most well-known horror of the Stalin era, Gulag is the Russian acronym for the Chief Administration of Corrective Labor Camps and Colonies. This complex network of forced labor camps and prisons was scattered throughout the Soviet Union. There were some 476 camps; the worst of them were in arctic or subarctic regions. Food was severely rationed, medical aid was next to none, clothing was inadequate, and torture was par for the course. Some of the camps were built by the prisoners themselves and run by ex-prisoners. Children born there were immediately seized and placed in orphanages.

While it is true that the Gulag contained the typical criminals—robbers, rapists, murderers—it was, most notably, the end of the line for political prisoners. Not all political prisoners were real opponents of Stalin and his policies; some of them were arbitrarily captured and charged as the secret police saw fit.

Upon Stalin's death in 1953, some of these camps were closed. Others, however, continued as forced labor camps for political prisoners until well into the 1980s. Today, the industrial towns of Norilsk, Vorkuta, Kolyma, and Magadan tell of their histories as Gulag camps.

Stalin is also the leader who led the Soviet Union into the Cold War against the West. His people lived in the darkness of isolation, relative poverty, and tyranny until his death in 1953.

Right: Holodomor monument in Kiev, Ukraine.

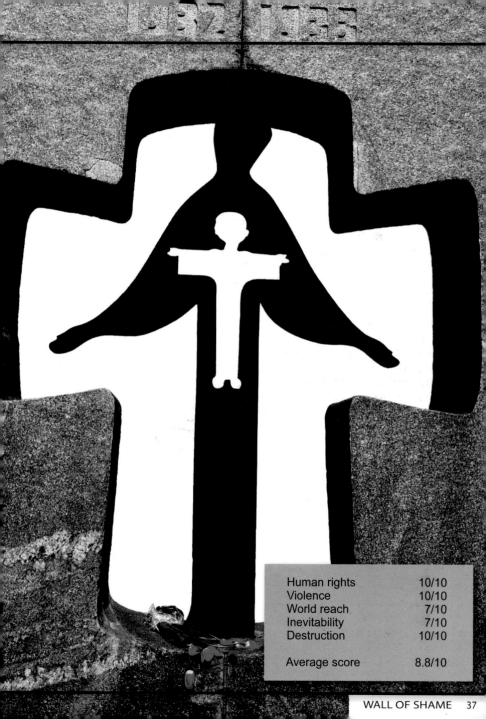

Human rights	10/10
Violence	10/10
World reach	7/10
Inevitability	7/10
Destruction	10/10
Average score	8.8/10

"They give you a gun and you have to kill the best friend you have. They do it to see if they can trust you. If you don't kill him, your friend will be ordered to kill you. I had to do it because otherwise I would have been killed. That's why I got out. I couldn't stand it any longer."
—*17-year-old Colombian boy who joined the paramilitary at age 7*

"They gave me a uniform and told me that now I was in the army. They even gave me a new name: 'Pisco.' They said that they would come back and kill my parents if I didn't do as they said."
—Former child soldier from DRC

According to the Coalition to Stop the Use of Child Soldiers, a child soldier is any person below 18 years of age who is, or who has been, recruited or used by an armed force or armed group in any capacity, including but not limited to children, boys and girls, used as fighters, cooks, porters, spies or for sexual purposes. It does not only refer to a child who is taking, or has taken, a direct part in hostilities. Over the world, thousands of children continue to be used as soldiers.

In Burundi, the *Forces Nationales pour la Libération,* an armed rebel Hutu group, recruited and forced hundreds of children between the ages of 10 and 16 to actively engage in military service.

In Côte d'Ivoire, children were recruited, often by force, to participate in armed conflict during the civil war of 2002. Both sides of the conflict abused the rights of children.

In the Democratic Republic of Congo, between the years of 2003 and 2006, more than an estimated 30,000 children, including young girls, were engaged in active warfare for the various rebel armies. We know this because Congolese and international aid workers actually removed these children and returned them to their civilian lives. The recruiting, however, continues. The various rebel armies are also responsible for kidnapping, abducting, maiming, raping, and committing other severe crimes against these children.

In Somalia, in 2004, reports published by the Coalition to Stop the Use of Child Soldiers claimed that over 200,000 children were part of that country's militia since 1991.

Opposite page: There are over 200,000 child soldiers in Africa.
Upper left and above: Military use of children in the Iran-Iraq war on the Iranian front.

In Sudan, military troops systematically recruit children into armed conflict. Young girls are threatened with rape until they enlist, and once enlisted are sexually abused regularly. Estimates are difficult to obtain, but reports show that over 16,000 children were forced into military action between 2001 and 2004.

In Uganda, human trafficking has included child soldiers and sex slaves for more than twenty years. The Rebel Lord's Resistance Army has forced more than 30,000 boys and girls into military service.

In Burma, boys as young as twelve years old are recruited into the national army. Many are forcibly recruited. Burma's official stance is that the minimum age is 18 and the army is voluntary; international analysis has found this to be false. Recruiters often coerce young children into the army as they leave their schools or get together with friends. There are cases of some of these young soldiers escaping to nearby Thailand.

In Iran, the Basij, the world's largest paramilitary force, recruits children on a regular basis. Iran's official policy on recruitment states that a child of sixteen can volunteer for military service but cannot serve in action until he is eighteen. It is known that many served on the frontlines of the Iran-Iraq war, where soldiers as young as twelve years old were killed.

In Sri Lanka, in May 2009, when Sri Lanka's thirty-year civil war ended, the government promised the United Nations to reintegrate thousands of child soldiers into society. President Mahinda Rajapakse reiterated his firm policy of zero tolerance in regard to child soldiers and has promised to cooperate with UNICEF for their release, surrender, and rehabilitation. UNICEF reports that some 5,666 children were abducted through the Liberation Tigers of Tamil Eelam.

In the United Kingdom, Canada, and the United States, children as young as sixteen (the UK) or seventeen (the USA and Canada) may join the military, with parental permission and under special conditions. In 2004, the Director of Military Personnel Policy for the U.S. Army acknowledged that almost sixty seventeen-year old soldiers were deployed to Iraq and Afghanistan in 2003-2004.

In Bolivia, a shocking 40 percent of the Bolivian army is believed to be under eighteen years of age. About half of these soldiers are under sixteen. The government is public on their forcible enlisting of children.

Human rights	10/10
Violence	8.5/10
World reach	8/10
Inevitability	9/10
Destruction	7.5/10
Average score	8.6/10

Right: Every year, thousands of children serve in the military in Democratic Republic of Congo.

Suspected nuclear weapons per country:

United States	10,500
Russia	10,000
France	464
China	410
Israel	200
United Kingdom	185
India	60
Pakistan	25
North Korea	?

Patrick Bonneville: I wonder if the political leaders and scientists who were working on nuclear arms were torn, knowing the result of their work would be mass destruction. Is the world a safer place with nuclear weapons? I am not convinced.

A nuclear weapon is a powerful explosive device that involves fission or fusion or a combination of both. Atomic bombs, or A-bombs, explode from the energy that is produced when a process of nuclear fission is detonated inside them. To create this reaction, fissile material, either uranium or plutonium, is assembled into a supercritical mass. The material is ignited through a "gun" method—shooting one piece of sub-critical material into another—or by compression, also known as the implosion method. The implosion method is considered the more sophisticated technology and is used when the bomb is made with plutonium.

The only country to have used nuclear weapons during wartime is the United States. On August 6, 1945, the USA dropped a uranium gun-type device code-named "Little Boy" on Hiroshima, Japan. Three days later, "Fat Man," a plutonium implosion device, was dropped on the Japanese city Nagasaki. The bombs caused the instant deaths of approximately 120,000 civilians, and the resulting radiation caused long-term illnesses that led to even more deaths.

Although the United States is the only country to have used these weapons against humanity, several countries admit to owning nuclear weapons. There have been over two thousand detonations during weapons testing and demonstrations. These countries are the Soviet Union, the United Kingdom, France, the People's Republic of China, India, Pakistan, and North Korea. It is believed that Israel also has nuclear weapons, but denies it. South Africa has renounced its independently developed nuclear weapons, and Belarus, Kazakhstan, and Ukraine all returned their Soviet-era nuclear weapons to Russia after the collapse of the USSR.

Above: Nagasaki bombing in World War II. The mushroom cloud resulting from the "Fat Man" explosion rose 18 km (11 mi, 60,000 ft) into the air.

There have been many treaties to restrict the development and use of nuclear weapons over the past forty years. The Treaty Banning Nuclear Weapon Tests in the Atmosphere, In Outer Space and Under Water—also known as the Partial Test Ban Treaty—was signed by the USSR, the UK, and the USA on August 6, 1963. Ratified by a vote of 80 to 19, it went into effect that same year and was opened to other countries to sign. Nevertheless, underground testing by all nuclear-known nations continued into the 1980s and '90s. North Korea announced plans to begin nuclear testing on May 25, 2009, and one month later threatened the United States, South Korea, and indeed the entire planet, with nuclear war. Peace is fragile.

The war-minded detonation of a nuclear bomb could destroy an entire city, kill millions of people, and endanger the natural environment for decades to come. Nuclear weapons also leave behind massive amounts of radiation after detonation. The effects of nuclear fallout threaten all forms of life and the environment. Direct exposure to high levels of radiation causes radiation burns and death, and long-term exposure to a radioactive environment causes birth defects and increased cancer rates.

With an estimated 26,000 nuclear weapons in existence around the world, the apathy of people in general with regard to nuclear armament seems

Above: Having now mastered nuclear power, Iran is closely monitored by the international community.

negligent. While the era of the backyard bomb-shelter is past, there is still plenty to be done by anti-nuclear activists.

"It's time to send a clear message to the world: America seeks a world with no nuclear weapons."
—U.S. President Barack Obama

""It was the balance of forces that preserved peace even during the Cold War."
—Russian Prime Minister Vladimir Putin

Human rights	10/10
Violence	2/10
World reach	10/10
Inevitability	10/10
Destruction	10/10
Average score	8.4/10

Patrick Bonneville: As the years go by, the Vietnam War becomes a distant memory for most of us. New generations, especially American and Vietnamese, learn about it in history books. It is important that we keep alive the lessons of this war. It divided America, much like the Iraq War has. There were many shameful acts perpetrated by both sides in this war, but the use of these chemical weapons strikes us as an element that is often forgotten.

The Vietnam War, which spilled across that country's borders into Laos and Cambodia, lasted some sixteen years. The communist North was supported by China and the Soviet Union, and South Vietnam was supported by the United States and members of the Southeast Asia Treaty Organization (SEATO – including Australia, France, Pakistan, the Philippines, Thailand and the United Kingdom). Statistics on this war vary depending on the source. According to the Vietnamese government, 1,100,000 military personnel from the Vietnam People's Army and the National Front for the Liberation of Vietnam were killed. Historians say the civilian casualties total closer to four million. The United States Armed Forces lost 58,209 members, while another 303,635 were wounded in action.

One of the many shameful elements of this war was the use of chemical agents in battle. Operation Ranch Hand, a U.S. military operation, took place from 1962 to 1971. During that time, more than 12 million U.S. gallons of chemical defoliants were sprayed over South Vietnam. The strategy was to kill the vegetation, and in so doing, kill the food chain and drive the communist Viet Cong out of the region.

Agent Pink, Agent Green, Agent Purple, Agent Blue, Agent White and Agent Orange were the chemicals of choice. Of these, only Agents Blue and White were free of dioxins. Dioxins are toxins that are known today to be carcinogenic; they also cause skin and respiratory diseases and birth defects. These effects were known to scientists before the use of the agents, and by the end of the invasion, 4.8 million Vietnamese people had been exposed. There were 400,000 related deaths and disabilities and an estimated 500,000 children born with birth defects. Today, almost half a century later, people living in affected regions still feel the effects, as many are born with genetic diseases.

Napalm is the name used to describe any number of flammable liquids used in warfare. It most often refers to jellied gasoline that actually sticks to surfaces. It is an American invention that saw light in 1942, at the hands of a team of chemists from Harvard University. Napalm kills or severely wounds by immolation or asphyxiation. Because it adheres to the skin, the heat of the fire immediately kills the nerve endings so victims often do not feel pain at the time. If a person doused in napalm does not die, second degree burns are not only painful, but leave the victim terribly scarred.

Many of us have seen the famous war photo of a young Vietnamese girl running naked down a village road. She is seen screaming—reportedly, she was crying, *"Nong qua!"* or "Too hot!" Her back was severely burned by napalm. Her name is Phan Thi Kim Phuc. The Associated Press photographer who took the photo, Nick Út, brought the girl and others hurt in that raid to a hospital in Siagon. She was so badly hurt, he was told, that she would not survive. He visited her often over the course of her fourteen-month hospitalization and her seventeen operations. Ms. Kim Phuc now lives with her husband and two children near Toronto, Ontario. She has since been awarded honorary university degrees, is a UNESCO Goodwill Ambassador, and runs a non-profit organization to aid children victims of war. Her message is one of forgiving, not forgetting.

"Before the war, I was never afraid. Then one day, the war started and it came to our village. I didn't even hear the explosion; I just saw the fire all around me. The pain was unbelievable. I would pass out every time the nurses put me in the burn bath. I almost died many, many times."
—*Phan Thi Kim Phuc, 2009*

"We should declare war on North Vietnam . . . We could pave the whole country and put parking strips on it, and still be home by Christmas."
—*Ronald Reagan, 1965, at the start of his political career*

Human rights	9/10
Violence	10/10
World reach	8/10
Inevitability	7/10
Destruction	7.5/10
Average score	8.3/10

Opposite page: Women and children among slain Viet Cong, May 1968.
Left: The U.S. Air Force and Navy heavily used napalm in Vietnam.

"In their greatest hour of need, the world failed the people of Rwanda."
—Kofi Annan

Patrick Bonneville: It is very hard to accept that this tragedy took place. The world knew about it but did nothing. Not much good came out of this ugly period of humanity, but when I look at General Roméo Dallaire, I know I can still believe in humankind. He saw the worst of what we imagine as hell and came away with courage. Another man, Paul Rusesabagina, from Kigali's Hôtel des Mille Collines, sheltered over a thousand refugees during the genocide. These two great men demonstrated that courage is stronger than fear. If we can learn something from this event, it is that we should all try to cultivate what Dallaire and Rusesabagina have: inner strength and compassion.

Rwanda, Africa, 1994: 10,000 people murdered every day; 400 every hour; 7 every minute. An estimated 800,000 were murdered from April to June, most of them Tutsis; some from a rival clan, the Hutus. The killing was triggered by the assassination of Rwandan President Juvenal Habyarimana, a Hutu.

Ten million Rwandans call this small landlocked country home. Known as *le pays des mille collines,* "land of a thousand hills," this country has the densest population in continental Africa. The land is home to the Twa—aboriginal Pygmy inhabitants—and to the Tutsis and the Hutus, two similar ethnic groups that speak the same language and follow the same traditions.

Left: Young Rwandan boy carrying his brother during their return from a refugee camp.
Right Bodies of Rwandans, 1994.

Understanding the Rwanda genocide requires an understanding of the country's recent history. After World War I, Belgium agreed to govern Ruanda-Urundi as stipulated in the League of Nations Mandate of 1923. Belgium also agreed to keep the existing class system of a minority Tutsi upper class and a lower class of both Hutus and Tutsi commoners. When Belgium decided to abolish the local government positions of "land-chief", "cattle-chief" and "military-chief," the Hutu were essentially cut off from holding any local power. By the end of the 1920s, the Hutu found themselves completely under Tutsi upper-class control.

Belgian and Roman Catholic Church authorities devised a way to segregate the ethnic races based on the number of cattle a person owned. Ten or more put the family in the aristocratic Tutsi class. Each citizen was issued an identity card clearly stating their ethnicity as "Tutsi," "Hutu," or "Twa." They also developed a segregated school system. When, later, the United Nations demanded a greater representation from the Hutu

population, the Tutsi monarchy demanded independence from Belgium. In their appeal for independence, they agreed to abolish the system of servitude.

In 1961, a general vote was held and the majority Hutu population elected to overturn the Tutsi monarchy. Years of guerrilla invasions from the neighboring Tutsi-controlled country, Burundi, generated mutual losses—in total, about 14,000 deaths. The following decade was painted with civil unrest and violence.

Tutsi refugees joined forces with a national resistance movement (RPF) during the Ugandan Bush War of the late 1980s. In 1990, the RPF invaded Rwanda and sought to oust the Hutu leaders. Each ethnic group, or clan, publicly called for the mistreatment of the other in their newspapers. The Hutu paper published the infamous "Hutu Ten Commandments," calling for Hutu supremacy in schools and the establishment of an exclusive Hutu army. In short, the Ten Commandments called for a retaliative suppression of the Tutsi people.

In August 1993, in an attempt to end civil war, the rebels and the Government of Rwanda signed the Arusha Accords peace treaty. President Juvenal Habyarimana's power was limited and transferred to the Transitional Broad Based Government (TBBG), which would combine the RPF and the five coalition parties in place. Not surprisingly, President Habyarimana's party was strongly opposed to sharing power and he refused to sign. When he made concessions, the RPF then refused. The situation was at a stalemate.

On April 6, 1994, a plane carrying Rwandan President Juvenal Habyarimana was shot down. It is generally believed that his own people, the Hutu, were upset by Habyarimana's signing of the Arusha Accord. Within hours of his death, violence exploded forth from the capital throughout the country. The following day, Prime Minister Agathe Uwilingiyimana prepared a radio address for the public but was killed by the President's guards before he could deliver it. The ten UN soldiers assigned to protect him were also murdered.

The genocide went on for three months. The Hutus ordered the mass slaughter of the Tutsi minority. Hutus were ordered to kill their Tutsi neighbors: government-sponsored radio broadcast the message, "You are with us and will massacre or you will be killed." Hutus were promised food or money or, in some cases, Tutsi land, for their participation. For the Tutsis, there was no help. The international community turned away from Rwanda after the murder of the ten UN soldiers.

Official figures published by the Rwandan government state that the death toll was an estimated 800,000 to 1,174,000. About 300,000 Tutsi survived and 400,000 children were orphaned. Thousands of women were raped and are now

HIV positive. Millions are believed to have fled to neighbouring Zaire, now the Democratic Republic of Congo. The speed with which pure violence and malice swept the country was unimaginable, even for people accustomed to civil war.

In July, the RPF captured Kigali, declared a ceasefire, and announced themselves victorious. The government collapsed. The first attempt at a multi-ethnic government failed, although eventually Paul Kagame was declared President. A French judge attributed the genocide to President Kagame, a notion he denies. Although the Rwandan civil war was over, the killing has continued in neighboring DR Congo.

The international community believed itself powerless to bring resolution to this situation- or so the powers that be would have us believe. Lieutenant General Roméo Dallaire, the United Nations Force Commander in Rwanda before the genocide, warned of plans by the Hutus to annihilate the Tutsis. His January 1994 telegram outlined information from an informant that gave a detailed account of the attack planned by the RPF in Kigali. Dallaire immediately drew up a plan to seize the arms and head off the attack but he was stopped. UN headquarters stated his actions were outside his mandate. He was allowed, instead, to advise President Habyarimana of the possible situation. Dallaire's requests to intervene and put an end to the situation, both before and during the genocide, were refused.

Despite their efforts, Lieutenant-General Dallaire and UN Assistance Mission for Rwanda were not able to stop the Hutus from executing their genocide. The official position from the United States was that this was not genocide; their involvement, therefore, was unnecessary. They would not interfere in "local conflict." It was a position the USA would later regret: then-President Bill Clinton would later publicly declare that if he had sent 5,000 peacekeepers, more than 500,000 lives could have been saved. He also apologized to the Rwandan people on two separate occasions, during visits to the country. He called his stance a "personal failure."

Today, the Rwandan government is still battling the consequences of the genocide. It must deal with the enormous challenge of reintegrating more than 2,000,000 refugees. It must deal with the long-term social effects of war rape, such as children from unwanted pregnancies and sexually transmitted diseases, including syphilis, gonorrhoea, and HIV/AIDS. Rwanda has also taken the constructive measures of creating policies denouncing discrimination based on ethnicity, race, or religion.

Human rights	10/10
Violence	10/10
World reach	4/10
Inevitability	9/10
Destruction	8/10
Average score	8.2/10

Patrick Bonneville: Eastern Asia was far from the world's thoughts after the end of the Vietnam War. But another chapter in humanity's dark story was being written. A new name began to be heard: Pol Pot, the leader of Cambodia's Khmer Rouge. His Communist Party ruled Cambodia with an iron fist. At least one-fifth of Cambodia's population died under Pol Pot's regime. And that doesn't include those who survived forced labor, torture, and the Khmer Rouge prisons.

Above: "Killing tree" in Choeung Ek Killing Fields, near Phnom Penh, Cambodia.
Right: Young Cambodian girl.

The Khmer Rouge would rule the country from 1975 to 1979. They would keep control in some isolated regions up to 1998. In 1968, Khmer Rouge forces launched a rebellion across Cambodia. It lasted for two years, until the Communist Party of Kampuchea (CPK) openly declared itself to be the government leader of Cambodia. In 1975, Pol Pot became the de facto leader of Cambodia—he was born Saloth Sar but adopted the name Pol Pot from the term *Politique Potentielle.* His campaign of terror against the Cambodian people caused an estimated 1.7 million deaths or 26 percent of the country's population. Some say that this figure is actually closer to 2.5 million.

Pol Pot's rise to power had been relatively slow, and he was not considered a force to be dealt with until the mid-70s. By 1973, in control of much of the country, he had drawn the attention of Vietnam. In order to preserve his power, he effectively cut the country

off from the international community and changed its name to "Democratic Kampuchea." In an effort to shore up his power, he first targeted Buddhist monks, Muslims, educated people, those with contacts outside the country—especially with Western countries or with Vietnam—the disabled, and the ethnic Chinese, Laotians, and Vietnamese. They were sent to the S-21 camp, where they were interrogated, tortured, and eventually killed. Pol Pot's extreme Maoist beliefs meant that he considered these city dwellers as a disease that must not infect Khmer Rouge territory.

The Khmer Rouge divided the population into three categories: full-rights people, candidates, and depositees. People were also classified according to ethnicity and religious beliefs, and it became illegal for them to speak their own ethnic languages or practice their customs. Depositees were "deposited" in villages in Pol Pot's Maoist drive to collectivize farming and build a

communist agricultural society. The depositees suffered beatings, were starved and forced to labor, and dug their own graves. These mass graves are now known as the "killing fields." Some victims were skinned alive, others burned alive. The Khmer Rouge declared that bullets were "not to be wasted" and abided by the credo, "to keep you is no benefit; to destroy you is no loss."

The conflict in Kampuchea, some say, was a direct result of the American bombing of areas close to the border of Vietnam. Their goal was to wipe out Vietnamese troops stationed there in the hopes of ending the Vietnamese War. Kampuchea retaliated. Taking control of Phnom Penh, the Khmer Rouge ordered the city evacuated under threat and gunpoint. This bustling capitol, often referred to as the Paris of Asia, was deserted. And so the violence and intimidation continued until, in 1979 Vietnam invaded Cambodia. Relying on a tactic referred to as the "Blooming Lotus," the Vietnamese military set out on three major highways into Phnom Penh. They took the city, forced Pol Pot into hiding and provoked the collapse of the Khmer Rouge. The Khmer Rouge continued, however, to govern the border region of Cambodia and Thailand until 1997, with apparent approval from the UN.

Today, Cambodia still struggles for peace. After several requests, the United Nations finally agreed to set up a tribunal to investigate charges of crimes against humanity and war crimes. In 2005, the Extraordinary Chambers in the Courts of Cambodia was created to operate as an independent court under Cambodian jurisdiction but based on international law. Five people are currently held and waiting trial. Four others are charged and remain under investigation.

The Tuol Sleng Genocide Museum in Phnom Penh is the actual site of Security Prison 21 (S-21). The seven survivors of the prison, as well as former personnel, say that about 40,000 innocent victims were tortured and murdered there. Pol Pot died while under house arrest in 1998; rumors still circulate that he was poisoned.

"I and everyone else who worked in that place knew that anyone who entered had to be psychologically demolished, eliminated by steady work, given no way out. No answer could avoid death. Nobody who came to us had any chance of saving himself."
—*Kang Kek Iew, Khmer Rouge leader of the Tuol Sleng (S-21) prison camp in Phnom Penh*

Human rights	10/10
Violence	10/10
World reach	4/10
Inevitability	8/10
Destruction	9/10
Average score	8.2/10

Right: Photographs of Khmer Rouge murder victims on display at Tuol Sleng Genocide Museum.

"The desperate plight of the people of Darfur has for too long been neglected or addressed with what the victims should rightly regard—and history will judge—as meek offerings, broken promises, and disregard."
—Ms. Louise Arbour, UN High Commissioner for Human Rights, on the occasion of the Fourth Special Session of the Human Rights Council, December 12, 2006

Patrick Bonneville: After the massacres in Rwanda and in Kosovo, we said we would never allow another genocide to take place. Not on our watch. Yet it has happened again, once more in Africa. Although events in Darfur are well-documented, it is shocking that they are not in the forefront of our media. Why are we allowing this violence, hatred, and killing to continue?

The word "genocide" was coined in the early 1940s. It is derived from the Greek word *géno(s)* meaning "race" and the Latin word *cide,* meaning "killing." It is the systematic and deliberate obliteration of an entire race, culture, or political group. The notion itself deserves a place on our Wall of Shame.

The United Nations and Amnesty International do not agree that the word "genocide" accurately describes what is happening in Darfur, a region of Sudan. Both organizations, however, strongly oppose the war and the obvious disregard for humanity that defines the actions of both the Sudanese government and rebel forces. The conflict has caused the deaths of some 300,000 to 450,000 Sudanese, and between 2.5 and 3.5 million people have been displaced.

Sudan is the largest country, by land size, in Africa. It is located in the northeastern area of the continent. According to the Sudanese government, its population is about 34 million; other sources say it is closer to 39 million. Arabic and English are the country's two official languages. Sudan gained its independence from colonial rule by the British and Egyptians in 1956. One year before gaining independence, a nasty civil war exploded between the North and the South—Arab and Muslim communities dominated the North; while the South, which wanted more autonomy, was Christian. Half a million people died because of this seventeen-year-war, which ended in 1972. A mere eleven years later, in 1983, civil war again inflamed the South, claiming some 1.9 million civilian lives. This civil war only officially ended in January 2005.

Meanwhile, in the far western side of the country, close to the border of Chad, the large province of Darfur saw another conflict arise in 2003. This civil war appears to be ethnic and economic rather than religious in nature, as the province is largely Muslim. All Darfuris are black Africans, and 35 percent of the population earn their living as nomadic herders. The remaining 65 percent is made up of sedentary farmers. Because of the desertification of the region and because of the growing population, tensions between the two groups has become fierce.

Oil also plays as important role in this conflict. Seventy percent of Sudan's revenue comes from this rich resource. Revenues are used to arm the national army and the Janjaweeds, or armed horse-mounted militias. China and Russia are the main importers of Sudanese oil, and they both have permanent seats on the United Nations Security Council. This may explain why international interventions have been limited.

In March 2003, the Sudan Liberation Army (SLA), along with the Justice and Equality Movement (JEM), engaged in conflict with government forces in Darfur. A few short months later, an estimated 65,000 refugees had escaped to neighboring Chad, and an estimated 500,000 civilians in Darfur were in dire need of humanitarian aid. On September 4, 2003, the SLA and the government reached a ceasefire agreement, but it wasn't long before each side accused the other of breaking it. All the while, UN agencies called for immediate humanitarian aid to be dispatched to the refugees in Chad.

In November of that same year, government-allied militias launched a reported six raids on camps near the Chad-Sudan border. One month later, Arab Janjaweed (meaning "genies on horseback") militias burnt villages, raped Darfuri women, and murdered civilians. This, in order to "clean up" Sudan on behalf of the government. Even more desperate Sudanese civilians fled to Chad.

Aid, however, was impossible to deliver. Borders and accesses were closed. Human rights violations were mounting. In April 2006, the SLA and JEM agreed to a forty-five-day ceasefire. Shortly after, the government signed a peace deal with the SLA but JEM rejected it. To further the peace and humanitarian aid process, the UK and the USA introduced a Security Council resolution at the United Nations, however Sudan rejected it almost immediately: they did not want any peacekeepers. The UN decided to send 22,500 troops and police to Darfur despite Khartoum's opposition. By early 2007, new talks of peace emerged as rebel groups and government took steps toward stopping the violence, but it didn't last for long. On March 31, 2007, Janjaweed militia in eastern Chad murdered at least sixty-five people, and as many as 8,000 civilians were displaced. Shamefully, the militia hid close to the refugee camps, waiting to finish the job.

The United Nations and non-governmental organizations played a crucial role in trying to keep refugees alive by providing basic needs: food, shelter, clothes, and medicine. The Sudan authorities made it difficult to deliver them, though. And Chad is worried about the rising number of refugees and the violence crossing into its borders. The United Nations and other NGOs estimated that casualties could rise to 100,000 deaths a month if this fragile aid structure were to collapse. There were about 13,000 aid workers doing everything they could in some 100 refugee camps spread over Darfur and Chad.

"On my recent trip, I once again held broken people in my arms, and once again they told me to tell the world that if something is not done, they will all die."
- Actress Mia Farrow, in her letter to U.S. President George W. Bush, May 28, 2008

Left: Omar Hassan Ahmad al-Bashir, the president of Sudan. An arrest warrant for al-Bashir was issued on March 4, 2009 for genocide, crimes against humanity and war crimes committed since 2003 in Darfur.

The Security Council of the United Nations finally agreed to authorize a real peacekeeping force with a mandate to protect Sudanese civilians. The African Union forces deployed in the region since October 2004 were not adequate for this challenge—they were underfunded, under-equipped, and exhausted. On August 31, 2006, the Security Council agreed to send about 20,600 individuals to replace the 7,000 African Union's force.

The day after the Security Council's decision, the Sudanese military responded by launching a major offensive in Darfur. The UN plan was suspended because of the Sudanese opposition. As a result, the exhausted African Union forces stayed. After months of diplomatic efforts at the United Nations, in June 2007, Sudan finally accepted a peace mission. On July 31, 2007, the Security Council unanimously authorized the establishment of UNAMID, the United Nations African Union Mission in Darfur, for an initial period of twelve months. The mission planned for a force of 19,555 military personnel and 6,432 police personnel. As of April 30, 2008, only 9,237 uniformed personnel were deployed.

"Thousands of villagers have reportedly fled their villages since 11 April after attacks by government forces and government-organized Arab militias fighting against the Sudan Liberation Army (SLA - formed in February by members of sedentary groups in the region) in the area of Kutum, in North Darfur."
—Amnesty International, April 28, 2003

"Would the world move in to stop it? My answer is I really don't know. I wish I could say yes but I am not convinced."
—Former United Nations Secretary-General Kofi Annan, commenting on world authorities stopping another genocide after the events of Rwanda in 1994

Human rights	10/10
Violence	10/10
World reach	5/10
Inevitability	8/10
Destruction	8/10
Average score	8.2/10

"In terrorism, one of the greatest targets of acts of terrorism is to make a society lose confidence in its government's capacity to protect its people."
—Abdelwahab Hechiche, professor of Government and International Relations at the University of South Florida

Patrick Bonneville: I think everyone, the world over, remembers exactly what they were doing on the Tuesday morning of September 11, 2001. The images and the sounds of the planes hitting New York's Twin Towers are written in our collective memory forever. The world stopped to watch the destruction of one of the great icons of capitalism. It was an act of terrorism fuelled by hate, extremism, and ideology. This event dug a wider gap between two worlds. In the West, it generated more racism against Muslims. And in the Middle East, it generated real war.

As New York City prepared for a regular autumn Tuesday, the unthinkable happened. Often referred to as 9/11, the events of September 11, 2001 were an organized terrorist attack by Al-Qaeda upon the United States. Nineteen hijackers took control of four passenger jets and intentionally crashed two of them into the Twin Towers of the World Trade Center in New York City, one into the Pentagon in Arlington, Virginia (just outside Washington DC), and the fourth into a field near Shanksville, Pennsylvania. The fourth plane had been redirected by the hijackers to Washington DC; however, we know that members of the flight crew and passengers tried to regain control of the aircraft just prior to its crash in a field.

The World Trade Center complex was a symbol of capitalism for the whole world. As the towers collapsed, flying debris caused the collapse of the nearby 7, World Trade Center building. It is known that about 2,500 toxic chemicals were released during the collapse. Emergency workers were called to rescue people, fight fires, tend to the wounded, and control the chaos. Four hundred and eleven emergency workers lost their lives in the line of duty: 341 firefighters; 2 NYFD paramedics; 23 police officers; 38 Port Authority Police officers; and 8 EMTS and paramedics from private emergency services.

In total, 2,974 people lost their lives because of these crashes. It is believed that 6,291 people were injured. The victims, representing over ninety different countries, were innocent people, going about their daily lives. Chaos, fear, shock, and horror swept the city, then around the country and the world.

The event ignited the United States' War on Terrorism: military operations were initiated by the United States and their allies to protect American citizens and business interests at home and abroad. The USA embarked on a plan to break up terrorist organizations within its borders and severely weaken international terrorist networks that operated under the command of Al-Qaeda. The USA proceeded to invade Afghanistan to dispose of the Taliban, who had harbored Al-Qaeda terrorists, and they opened their Guantanamo Prison to interrogate terrorist suspects. The USA Patriot Act, national anti-terrorist legislation, was enacted by its legislators.

Right: New York City, September 11, 2001.

WALL OF SHAME   69

In immediate response to the attacks, the U.S. Federal Aviation Administration (FAA) immediately grounded all flights and re-routed arrivals to Canada. During this operation, 255 flights were diverted to fifteen different airports across Canada. The FBI was also fast to respond: within a few hours, names and even personal details of the suspected hijackers emerged. One of the men, Mohamed Atta, had checked a bag that morning that missed its flight. It contained papers that listed a terrorist team of nineteen men and their plans, motives, and background. Both the U.S. National Security Agency and German intelligence agencies intercepted communications that pointed to Osama bin Laden.

The FBI released photos of the nineteen hijackers and related information two weeks later. Fifteen of the men were from Saudi Arabia, two from the United Arab Emirates, one from Egypt, and one from Lebanon. Mohamed Atta, whose suitcase missed the flight, was the leader of the group. They were all well-educated adults.

Plans for the attacks had been detailed in an Al-Qaeda statement issued by Osama bin Laden, Ayman al-Zawahiri, Ahmed Refai Taha, Mir Hamzah, and Fazlur Rahman in 1998. The statement clearly quoted the Qur'an: "Slay the pagans wherever ye find them." The statement interpreted this message to mean it is the "duty of every Muslim to kill Americans anywhere."

Left: September 11 memorial, made from twisted steel beams on an empty beach.

In his 2002 "Letter to America", bin Laden wrote: "You are the worst civilization witnessed by the history of mankind: You are the nation who, rather than ruling by the Sharia of Allah in its Constitution and Laws, choose to invent your own laws as you will and desire. You separate religion from your policies, contradicting the pure nature which affirms Absolute Authority to the Lord and your Creator."

The world reacted against Muslims. Hate crimes flourished in the days following September 11. Middle Eastern nationals, and even people who simply looked Middle Eastern were victims of harassment. There were physical and verbal attacks and vandalism on Islamic religious buildings, and there was at least one known murder: Blabir Singh Sodhi was shot on September 15, 2001—he was a Sikh mistaken for a Muslim.

The September 11 attacks also affected the American economy: an estimated 430,000 jobs and $2.8 billion in wages were lost in the three months following the events. The U.S. Federal government provided $21.7 billion dollars in aid to the city of New York for economic development and infrastructure needs.

Human rights	8/10
Violence	9/10
World reach	8/10
Inevitability	7/10
Destruction	9/10
Average score	8.2/10

Patrick Bonneville: Israel. Iraq. Afghanistan. Pakistan. Jordan. Lebanon. Sri Lanka. India. Russia. United States. Turkey. Tanzania. Kenya. United Kingdom. Yemen. Suicide attacks take place all over the globe. The people killed by suicide bombs are fathers, mothers, sons and daughters. There are other ways to fight, other ways to be heard.

Yet, in the last two decades, suicide attacks against civilians have skyrocketed. There were five to ten such attacks per year in the 1980s. There are currently between 300 and 500 a year. Israel, Iraq, Afghanistan, and Sri Lanka have undergone suicide attacks. Nor can the world forget the "Suicide Bomber" headlines from Beirut, London, Paris, Madrid, Mumbai, Jerusalem, Tel-Aviv, Baghdad, and Moscow. Not to mention New York City.

Some recent suicide bombings around the world:

March 27, 2002
The Passover Massacre was a suicide bombing in Netanya, Israel, during a Passover meal. The dinner was being attended by Holocaust survivors. Hamas, the Palestinian Islamic resistance movement, claimed responsibility. Thirty Israeli civilians were killed, one hundred and forty were injured.

August 9, 2001
The Sbarro Restaurant Bombing was a Palestinian attack on a pizzeria in downtown Jerusalem, Israel. Fifteen civilians, including seven children, were killed. Another 130 were injured.

The suicide bomber attacked at about two o'clock in the afternoon, when the restaurant and surrounding streets would be bustling with activity.

January 29, 2004
A suicide bomber boarded an Egged bus, a Jerusalem bus line that is often targeted. Eleven civilians were killed, fifty wounded. The blast was timed for nine o'clock in the morning, at a stop outside Prime Minister Ariel Sharon's official residence.

February 6, 2004
The Moscow Metro Bombing was a suicide attack that killed 40 people and injured 120 others.

March 11, 2004
The Madrid Train Bombings, also known as 3/11, were a series of orchestrated bombings just three days before Spain's general elections. The attacks were inspired by Al-Qaeda terrorism, although no direct link to Al-Qaeda has been proven. A total of 191 people were killed and another 1,800 injured. Ten explosions rocked the train systems during the Thursday morning rush hour. Three other bombs were successfully detonated.

July 7, 2005
The London Bombings, also known as 7/7, were a series of suicide attacks on London's public transit system during the morning rush hour. The criminals were British Muslims incensed by Britain's involvement in the Iraq War. Their actions cost the lives of 52 people and injured 700.

Right: Muslim women have committed many suicide bombings in the past few years.

November 9, 2005

The Amman Bombings killed 60 people and injured 115. The attacks focused on three hotels in Amman, Jordan, and responsibility is believed to belong to Islamic terrorists. Three bombers killed themselves; a fourth—a woman and wife of one of the dead bombers—did not succeed in her attempt, as her bomb-loaded belt failed to trigger. She was arrested and executed in September 2006.

July 11, 2006

The Mumbai Train Bombings were a series of seven bomb detonations over the course of eleven minutes in the subway system of Mumbai (Bombay), India. These attacks killed 209 people and injured 700 others. Mumbai police claim the attacks were the actions of Lashkar-e-Toiba and the Students' Islamic Movement of India (SIMI). To date, up to 300 people have been detained in connection to the bombings. In February 2009, detained Indian Mujahideen leader Sadiq Sheikh confessed to participating in the attacks.

October 18, 2007

The Karachi Bombing was an assassination attempt on former Pakistani Prime Minister Benasir Bhutto. Although she survived, 139 innocent civilians did not. The bombing injured another 450. The majority of the murdered were members of the Pakistan Peoples Party. Blame for the attacks flew back and forth between Islamic terrorists and the ruling party. No one has claimed responsibility.

July 7, 2008

The Indian Embassy Bombing in Kabul, Afghanistan, killed 58 people and injured 141. The bombing occurred as people were lining up to obtain visas for entry to India. No one group has claimed responsibility, and although the Taliban denied involvement, they issued a statement claiming they would have liked to be responsible. India, Afghanistan, and Pakistan all denied involvement.

February 2, 2008

Two mentally disabled women were used as guinea pigs in attacks in Baghdad. Explosives were attached to the women who were then sent into busy markets. The explosives were ignited by remote control. At least 98 people were killed and another 200 wounded.

January 22, 2007

Baghdad plays host yet again to a terrorist attack that killed 88 people. In fact, since 2003, Iraqi civilians have been regular targets of suicide warfare. A 2005 Human Rights Watch report noted, "The groups that are most responsible for the abuse, namely Al-Qaeda in Iraq and its allies, Ansar al-Sunna and the Islamic State of

Iraq, have all targeted civilians for abductions and executions. The first two groups have repeatedly boasted about massive car bombs and suicide bombs in mosques, markets, bus stations and other civilian areas. Such acts are war crimes and in some cases may constitute crimes against humanity, which are defined as serious crimes committed as part of a widespread or systematic attack against a civilian population."

February 3, 2007
A large truck bomb was detonated in the heart of a Baghdad market. At least 135 people were killed and 339 injured. The bomb brought down at least ten buildings and coffee shops and destroyed the better part of the largely Shi'ite neighborhood.

August 19, 2003
A bomb hit the newly opened United Nations Assistance Mission in Iraq, killing the UN Special Representative for Iraq, Sérgio Vieira de Mello. A second bomb a month later forced the withdrawal of UN staff members and had a profound effect on peace efforts.

June 9, 2009
A bomb at the Pearl Continental Hotel in Peshawar, Pakistan, killed 17 people, including Perseveranda So, the Chief of Education for UNICEF in Pakistan. Ms. So was in Peshawar to help implement educational programs for girls. The blast also killed Mr. Aleksandar Vorkapic, the UN High Commissioner for refugees. Two unknown groups claimed responsibility: Fedayeen al-Islam said they were

protesting against U.S. interference in Pakistan; Abdullah Azzam Shaeed Brigade said they were retaliating against the Pakistani military attacks on the Taliban in the Swat Valley.

Above: Workers and soldiers search through the rubble of UN headquarters in Baghdad, after the building was attacked by suicide bombers on August 19, 2003.

"Nothing can excuse this act of unprovoked and murderous violence against men and women who went to Iraq for one purpose only: to help the Iraqi people recover their independence and sovereignty, and to rebuild their country as fast as possible, under leaders of their own choosing."
—Kofi Annan, following the suicide bombing against the UN in Iraq

Human rights	10/10
Violence	10/10
World reach	8/10
Inevitability	4/10
Destruction	8/10
Average score	8.0/10

Patrick Bonneville: When the New World was discovered and colonized, the people native to these lands suffered at the hands of the colonizers. And throughout Africa, Asia, Oceania, and in some remote regions of Europe, indigenous people have also seen their cultures and their lives shattered. Today, the leaders of countries who bear responsibility for that devastation are called upon to admit the legacy of suffering their ancestors left behind. Honoring indigenous peoples, their cultures and rich roots, can only strengthen our world by bringing us together and eliminating barriers.

The UN estimates that there are more than 370 million indigenous people in about 70 countries worldwide. In September 2007, the UN General Assembly adopted the Declaration on the Rights of Indigenous Peoples. Four countries—all of them with significant indigenous populations—voted against the declaration: the United States, Canada, New Zealand, and Australia. Thirty-four nations abstained from voting to ratify the declaration: Azerbaijan, Bangladesh, Bhutan, Burundi, Colombia, Georgia, Kenya, Nigeria, Russia, Samoa, and Ukraine. One hundred and forty-three countries voted in favor.

Here is an overview of only some of the sordid history of oppression of indigenous people in some countries:

Right: Maori totem with facial tattoo markings, Marahau, Nelson District, New Zealand.

Australia

From 1869 to roughly 1969, Australian federal and state agencies, in concert with church missions, separated aboriginal children from their families in a project of assimilation. They were children of Australian Aborigines and Torres Strait Islander ethnic groups. These children are referred to as the Stolen Generations or the Stolen Children.

New Zealand

During the white settlement of New Zealand, armed conflicts arose over the immigrants' sale and confiscation of land belonging to the Māori. Between 1845 and 1872, under the New Zealand Settlements Act, land was systematically distributed amongst the white population as a form of supposed punishment for native rebellion. In reality, friend or foe, Māori land was taken away without their consent. During the New Zealand Wars, more than four million acres (16,000 km²) of land were confiscated. This had enduring negative effects on the Māori people and their social and economic development. Eventually, about half of the stolen land was returned or paid for, although it was often not returned to its original owners.

Mali/Algeria/Niger

Over the course of several battles, Tuareg groups resisted French colonial invaders. The Tuareg could not, however, compete with the sophisticated weapons held by the French, and they were forced to surrender. Tuareg tribes were subdued and required to sign treaties.

Democratic Republic of Congo

At the 2003 UN Indigenous Peoples' Forum, participants listened to the horrors endured by the Mbuti pygmies. Their representative, Sinafasi Makelo, described how his people were hunted down and eaten during the Congo Civil War by a North Kivu group known as *Les Effaceurs,* "the erasers." The Mbuti were considered "subhuman" and their flesh, when eaten, was believed to instill magical powers. Minority Rights Group International has urged the International Criminal Court to investigate what they believe to be an organized crusade of extermination by the transitional government's Movement for the Liberation of Congo. Although much of the evidence of this horrific violence points to the Movement, rebel forces from various sides are just as guilty of these crimes.

Canada

Federal policy in early Canada was focused on the assimilation of indigenous groups with the European settlers. The idea was to control the land in totality. In order to do this, the government simply created amendments to the Indian Act in 1905 and 1911, making it even easier to displace First Nations People and claim their land. Tactics such as withdrawal or retention of funding were used to manipulate populations into relenting. In 1912, the province of British Columbia created the McKenna-McBride Royal Commission to settle land ownership disputes. Claims from indigenous groups were largely ignored and resulted in the relocation of many First Nations people to less valuable areas known as "reserves."

The residential school system was founded to force the assimilation of indigenous children into white society. Beginning around 1928, the government began separating children from their families and placing them in church-run, government-funded residential schools. The result was decades of physical, sexual, and emotional abuse.

United States

On May 26, 1830, President Andrew Jackson signed into law the practice of "civilizing" the Native Americans. Many were relocated as their land was confiscated to allow for American industry to evolve. The mass movement of these ethnic groups is often referred to as the "Trail of Tears." European diseases, starvation, and exposure led to the death of thousands, including 4,000 of the 15,000 displaced Cherokee.

Brazil

The Yanomami is possibly the largest and oldest native tribe worldwide. Its people have lived for thousands and thousands of years with deep respect for their land and culture. Since the 1980s, after the discovery of gold on their traditional lands, their way of life has been under threat. In 1977, the population was 20,000, but after the arrival of gold miners, the figure dropped dramatically, to about 9,000. Speculators not only destroy the ecosystem as they excavate for gold, they also bring disease, pollution, and poisons as yet unknown the area. Mercury, used to extract deposits from rivers, is killing the fish, and tuberculosis, malaria, and the flu are killing thousands of Yanomami. Government intervention has brought some protection, and the population is recovering slowly. Nevertheless, influences from the outside world have already left a terrible scar on the culture and the lifestyle of this ancient people.

Norway – Sami

The Sami culture has been present in Norway, Sweden, Finland and in small pockets of Russia for the last 2,500 years. The first ethnic group to establish roots in these areas, they are considered indigenous. The Sami people of Norway were reindeer herders and fishermen. They were largely nomadic, following the migration paths of the reindeer. As Norway became home to sedentary European settlers, the two groups remained separate. With 1349's Black Plague, a considerable percentage of Norway's population was wiped out. The Sami were mostly spared from the illness. Eventually, the Norwegian government soon recognized the loss in tax revenue and came up with a plan: convince the Sami to move to the abandoned farms and begin a new way of life. The nomadic Sami all but disappeared. At the beginning of the twentieth century, Sami had to speak Norwegian in order to obtain land. There are nine Sami dialects; today, of these, one is probably extinct, fewer than twenty people can speak two others, and the other six are in danger. Norway is now trying to make amends.

Peru

Prior to the arrival of European explorers, there were an estimated 2,000 native nations in the Peruvian region. Today, there are about twenty-one. Either through assimilation or genocide, the bulk of Peru's indigenous population has been wiped out. In the span of about 100 years—from 1520 to 1620—the population of nine million strong dwindled to a mere 600,000. Those who remain continue to fight for their land and culture. Their biggest fight is against foreign mining and forestry companies, whose exploitation destroys the ecosystem and the local indigenous way of life.

Alan García is the current president of Peru. His administration is in the middle of a battle over oil in the lands of indigenous people throughout the country. Representatives of these ethnic groups say that their very lives are at stake. They report being shot at from helicopters and from the ground, and they are fearful that local food resources will be removed or destroyed. The police are accused of burning bodies to hide the number of casualties. As of June 9, 2009, the president still refused to meet with indigenous leaders for open communication and resolution.

Human rights	10/10
Violence	8/10
World reach	8/10
Inevitability	9/10
Destruction	2/10
Average score	7.4/10

PAZI - MINE

ПАЗИ - МИНЕ

Patrick Bonneville: This region has a long history of hate and suffering. It was at the center of World War I, and it exploded into crisis again just a few years ago. After the fall of the Berlin Wall, it was just a matter of time before the situation ignited, lessons from the last World Wars quickly forgotten. The country was marked by too many differences. Some wanted control, others revenge. The breakup of Yugoslavia came at a very high price. Families, lives, and cities were destroyed. The word genocide started to appear again.

The dissolution of the Socialist Federal Republic of Yugoslavia entailed a decade of conflict, from 1991 to 2001. Yugoslavia had a history riddled with political crisis, war, and ethnic violence. The republic included Slovenia, Croatia, Bosnia and Herzegovina, Macedonia, Montenegro, Serbia, and within Serbia were Kosovo and Vojvodina—each with its own rich history.

Left: A red mine alert sign in Bosnia and Herzegovina.
Above: Remains of the 1984 Sarajevo Olympics.
Upper right: An exhumed mass grave in Potocari, Bosnia and Herzegovina, where key events in the July 1995 Srebrenica Massacre unfolded.

The ethnic groups who clashed were, depending on the geographic area in question, Serbs, Croats, Bosniaks, and Albanians. Today, the results of the wars are poverty, economic collapse, and instability. The wars were bloody, and the International Criminal Tribunal for the former Yugoslavia was created to prosecute those charged with war crimes.

Fighting began almost immediately upon the declarations of independence of Slovenia and Croatia in 1990. It would not stop for the next eleven years. Slovenia's departure from the federation, which had been pretty much expected, was quick and less violent than what would follow in Croatia. In 1992, the United Nations and the European Union recognized Slovenia as an independent country.

The Croatian population was not so lucky. In 1992, the UN recognized Croatia as an independent state; however from 1991 to 1995, the region was bathed in blood as war raged between Croatian police forces and Serbs living in the Socialist Republic of Croatia. Croatia elected a non-Communist government, the Serbs a Communist government. The Serbs quickly gathered an impressive military force which had access to a large Croatian arsenal. In the end, the Croats lost valuable coastal land, inland territories, and important cities. They also lost thousands of lives. Sources put the amount of people displaced between 200,000 and 300,000. The UNPROFOR, a UN protection force, was established to support peace in the region.

Land the Serbs had seized—about 30 percent of the former Yugoslav Republic of Croatia—would remain under their control. Croat civilians remaining in this territory were subjected to looting, rape, and murder.

The ethnic cultures that make up the regions of Bosnia and Herzegovina were desperate to each claim a portion of that land and to claim their subsequent independence. It was soon realized, though, that no one group could out-battle the Serbs. So, under threat of annihilation, the people of Bosnia and the people of Herzegovina joined forces to fight the Serbs. The three years of ethnic cleansing that followed left behind 97,207

identified victims, and possibly more. An estimated 1.8 million people were displaced.

While these parts of the former Yugoslavia were in conflict, another ethnic group, the Albanians, were growing progressively uneasy about the increased power held by the Serbs. This group occupied a region known as Kosovo, which the Serbs considered to be the cradle of their culture and traditions. In 1996, an organized attack on Serbian security personnel was carried out, seemingly out of nowhere. An unknown political group called the Kosovo Liberation Army (KLA) claimed responsibility. Members of the KLA were farmers and unemployed people. As tensions grew, the KLA was viewed as a terrorist organization by the government and as freedom fighters by the Albanian population. The U.S. government listed the KLA as terrorists and linked them to Osama bin Laden, a declaration they would later renounce.

Left: Kosovar refugees fleeing their homeland.
Above: Slobodan Milosevic, president of the Federal Republic of Yugoslavia, was accused of genocide, crimes against humanity, and violations of the customs of war.

"A Serb told the mother to make the child stop crying. But when the baby continued to cry, he took it from the mother and slit its throat. Then he laughed."
—Munira Subasic, Srebenica survivor

By 1998, the KLA was strong and the Serbs set out to crush the group. The international community stepped in with hopes of helping the formation of an accord for peace, which the Albanians accepted and the Serbs did not. NATO began to bomb strategic posts on both sides. After eleven weeks of bombing, the Serbs withdrew. Almost immediately, an estimated 750,000 Albanian refugees poured back into Kosovo while about 100,000 Serbs fled.

Now the UN had to decide if Kosovo should be considered Serbian, or independent. They began to investigate Serbian crimes against humanity, and Serbian leader Slobodan Milosevic became the first serving head of state to be charged and indicted for crimes against humanity by the International War Crimes Tribunal. Milosevic and a number of his colleagues were found to be responsible for the deportation of an estimated 750,000 Kosovar Albanians and the murder of some 600 others. In February 2008, the government of Kosovo declared independence from Serbia, igniting more debate and fear worldwide. While some members of the United Nations recognize this independence, others do not. Serbia has threatened decreased cooperation with those that do. In order to have an independent view on the situation, the UN has asked the International Court of Justice to review the validity of the declaration.

The attacks known as the Southern Serbia Conflict took place between June 1999 and November 2000. There were 294 attacks in which dozens of civilians lost their lives. The aim of the conflict was to expand the region of Kosovo. The attacks did not garner the international attention the perpetrators were seeking, and as a result, they ceased fire in November 2000.

The final battle in the break-up of Yugoslavia was the Macedonia conflict. During most of 2001, ethnic Albanians of the National Liberation Army (NLA) staged planned attacks.

Although loss of life was not great during this particular conflict, the tension between the ethnic states was. Several leaders were charged with war crimes, including burning hostages alive.

""I deeply regret the death of Slobodan Milosevic. It deprives the victims of the justice they need and deserve."
—ICTY Chief Prosecutor Carla Del Ponte

Human rights	9/10
Violence	8.5/10
World reach	8/10
Inevitability	7/10
Destruction	7/10
Average score	7.9/10

"We cannot ignore the fact that thousands of Chechen civilians have died and more than 200,000 have been driven from their homes. Together with other delegations, we have expressed our alarm at the persistent, credible reports of human rights violations by Russian forces in Chechnya, including extrajudicial killings. There are also reports that Chechen separatists have committed abuses, including the killing of civilians and prisoners..."
—United States Secretary of State Madeleine Albright, March 24, 2000

Patrick Bonneville: The Chechen wars caused great suffering for civilians on both sides. The main issue: independence. What might have been a flourishing region or country has been torn apart. Because of this conflict, in September 2004, humanity reached a new low. Parents from all around the world shared the grief of Beslan's fathers and mothers when, on September 1, children paid for our craziness once again.

Independence is a cry that has been heard in every corner of the world throughout the course of human history. It is a fundamental human right, yet it is so easily removed. Human beings do not take kindly to their freedoms being stolen, repressed, or destroyed. War is often the result of a desire for independence, a desire for the freedom of one's people, of one's nation.

This was the story of Chechnya from 1994 to 1996. The First Chechen War was fought between the Russian Federation and the Chechen Republic of Ichkeria, when Russian forces tried to secure and control a mountainous area surrounding the region. They failed. Despite their inflated military personnel, immense weaponry, and their air support, Chechen guerrillas maintained control. In 1996, Russian leader Boris Yeltsin declared a ceasefire. The number of Russian deaths varies, depending on the sources, with some saying as little as 3,500 and others claiming over 14,000. Chechen figures are similar, with estimates between 3,000 and 15,000. Civilian deaths, however, total over 100,000. Another 200,000 civilians were injured, and as many as 500,000 were displaced. One could almost say that the first Chechen war succeeded only in killing thousands and destroying the lives of tens of thousands more.

The Second Chechen War began in 1999 with an armed invasion of Dagestan by a group of Chechnya-based militants. The short-lived siege marked the end of the independence of the Chechen Republic of Ichkeria. Terrorist attacks on civilians and widespread human rights violations drew condemnation from the international community. Russia demobilized the Chechen rebel movement and the fighting has all but ceased. Their army no longer patrols the streets and the destroyed city of Grozny has been rebuilt. This war cost the lives of some 50,000 civilians and as many as 11,000 soldiers. Tens of thousands of non-Chechen ethnic citizens had fled the country for fear of violence and discrimination.

Above: Russian tanks move into the mountain regions of Chechnya, in the First Chechen War.
Right: Map of the Chechen Republic.

The long civil war saw human rights abuses in disturbing numbers: innocent people killed and entire villages destroyed. Environmental agencies warned of an ecological disaster in the form of oil spills, chemical and radioactive pollution, loss of wildlife terrain, and loss of forests. Added to these hazards, land mines scatter the region. Chechnya, today, has the most land mines on the entire planet.

In one of the most frightening acts of war, 1,100 people at School Number One (SNO) in Beslan, Russia, were taken hostage on September 1, 2004. Of these, 777 were children. The Beslan School Siege was planned by a group of armed terrorists led by Shamil Basayev, an independent warlord. They deemed that the best way to show the desperation of their struggle against Russia was to invade this school and create hell on earth for the students and teachers inside. The infuriating paradox of their manifesto—to end the war by attacking the innocent—pushed them to kill at least 334 of these hostages, including 186 children. Hundreds more were wounded. Basayev's Riyadus-Salikhin Reconnaissance and Sabotage Battalion of Chechen Martyrs claimed responsibility.

Secret negotiations had been underway between the terrorists and several government officials, both locally and nationally. An offer was made to replace the 700 children with 700 adult volunteer hostages. But, by the third day, patience was wearing thin and the true attack began. On September 3, in the early afternoon, the rebels opened fire and detonated two explosions. At least half of the hostages burned to death in the subsequent fire.

For its own role in the carnage of the Chechen wars, Russia's Chechnya was placed on the Genocide Watch List in 2001 by the United States Holocaust Memorial Museum. The museum claims that the Russian state has a history of persecuting the Chechens as a people, of demonizing Chechens as a group within Russian society, and of exercising an inordinate amount of violence against Chechen civilians by Russian armed forces.

Human rights	9/10
Violence	9/10
World reach	4/10
Inevitability	7.5/10
Destruction	8.5/10
Average score	7.6/10

Patrick Bonneville: We understand that Israel needs to protect itself and its population. We are not critical of Israel's existence. But bombing and targeting civilian areas, schools, and hospitals cannot be justified. In battles in 2006 and 2008, too many innocent people lost their lives because of Israeli force. For the sake of generations to come, for the sake of the world, this very small country must find a way to create some kind of peaceful co-existence with ts neighbors.

This part of the Middle East has been riddled with conflict through the ages and up to recent history. A 34-day military conflict took place between Lebanon and northern Israel in 2006. During the strike, Israel made use of cluster bombs. The conflict killed over 1,000 people, mostly Lebanese civilians. About one million Lebanese were displaced as well as an estimated 300,000 to 500,000 Israelis.

In the Gaza War of 2008, part of the ongoing Israeli-Palestinian conflict, Israel's Operation Cast Lead's mission was to stop Hamas rocket attacks on southern Israel as well as arms smuggling into the region. The Israeli Air Force bombed Hamas military bases, training camps, and Kassam launchers. In the Gaza Massacre that December, bombing attacks began as school was let out for the day. The Gaza attacks left 1,417 Palestinians killed, of whom 313 were children. The number of wounded civilians is also staggering: over 5,000. Once the assaults ended, thirteen nations worldwide, including the United States, expressed support for Israel by recognizing the country's right to defend itself.

"Israel fired huge numbers of cluster bombs into Lebanon, leaving bomblets that have killed and maimed almost 200 people since the war ended. Only a global treaty that bans cluster munitions will prevent such tragedies in the future."
—Steve Goose, Director of Human Rights Watch Arms Division

Above: Israeli soldier taking a break.
Right: Israeli tank coming out of the Gaza, and blowing up sand like waves.
Opposite page: Deadly borders.

LES PHOTOS DU CARNAGE
aza martyr

LES PHOTOS DU CARNAGE

COMBATS MEURTRIERS DANS GAZA

«C'est la Palestine
qu'il faut sauver»

C'est le cri d'alarme lancé par Leïla Shahid
et des personnalités françaises.
Malgré tous les appels internationaux au cessez-le-feu,
Israël poursuit son agression.
Seules des sanctions peuvent stopper le massacre.
PAGE 2

During these two recent wars, Israel used white phosphorus, a chemical compound that, when released, creates a smokescreen that can shield an army. Particles from the chemical adhere to the skin and burrow into the body, where the phosphorus enters vital organs. White phosphorus is extremely flammable and difficult to extinguish; it continues to burn until it is deprived of oxygen. The use of the chemical is not new or illegal, however it is highly controversial. Human Rights Watch published an exhaustive report on the use of white phosphorus by the Israeli military on March 25, 2009. This report proves that the chemical was used on civilian homes, schools, buildings, and entire neighborhoods. A United Nations zone was also attacked. At least ten civilians suffered extreme burns due to white phosphorus. As a result, Human Rights Watch declared Israel's use of the chemical illegal.

Left: Over 1,400 Palestinians were killed in the 2008 Gaza War, including more than 400 children and women.
Above: Mortars flash in the night sky above Gaza.

"The Commissioner-General of UNRWA, Karen AbuZayd, expressed her horror to the extensive destruction visited upon Gaza Strip today and her deep sadness to the terrible loss in human life. UNRWA, the United Nation's Relief and Works Agency for Palestine Refugees, strongly urges the Israeli Government to heed calls for ceasing its bombardment on Gaza. Israel is a signatory to international conventions that protect non-combatants in times of conflict. These conventions are worthless if they are not upheld."
—United Nation's Relief and Works Agency for Palestine Refugees, December 27, 2008

"The use of air-dropped incendiary weapons against military objectives within a concentration of civilians is simply prohibited. These prohibitions are contained in Protocol III of the Convention on Certain Conventional Weapons."
—Peter Herby, head of the International Committee of the Red Cross's Arms Unit

Human rights	9/10
Violence	9/10
World reach	3/10
Inevitability	8/10
Destruction	9/10
Average score	7.6/10

Patrick Bonneville: Nowadays, for those in the West, segregation seems to be part of a horrible old story. We cannot forget we finished one of these dark chapters not so long ago. In South Africa, the scars are still fresh. In 1994, the people of South Africa, blacks and whites together, ended apartheid, one of the ugliest moments of modern humanity.

South Africa has a population of about 48 million people. Of them, 79.5 percent are Black, 9.2 percent are White, 8.9 percent are Coloured (mixed races), and 2.5 percent are Asian. Apartheid, a National Party government policy of racial segregation, was ruthlessly practiced in South Africa from 1948 until 1994.

During the apartheid era, these four racial groups were stringently defined. In cases of uncertainty regarding classification, the "pencil test" provided clarification. If a person's hair was kinky enough for a pencil to get stuck, the person was to be labeled "Black."

These criteria were explained in the Population Registration Act.

Apartheid is an Afrikaans word that means "separateness." Afrikaaners, settlers of mostly Dutch origins, had colonized the country during the seventeenth and eighteenth centuries. In 1948, Blacks were stripped of their citizenship and became second-class citizens overnight. Although the government provided basic medical and education services, they were inferior to services offered to Whites. Blacks had been obligated for decades to carry their identity cards at all times and their movements were restricted. Without permission and a signed pass, a Black person simply could not move about at will.

The National Party had very specific White supremacist policies, including the 1949 Prohibition of Mixed Marriages Act. The 1950 Immorality Act, in which sexual relations between persons of different races were criminalized. The 1950 Group Areas Act, which partitioned land to allocated racial groups. The 1953 Reservation of Separate Amenities Act, which legislated public segregation: Whites and Blacks were to use separate amenities.

Left: 79% of the South African population is black.
Above: Mourners carrying coffins of victims of the South African police at Langa Township in Uitenhage.
Right: White police with dogs guard the grounds at the new Ellis Park Stadium, Johannesburg, 1982.

These and numerous other racist acts were passed over the next few decades. They included acts permitting discrimination according to race in employment situations, acts that created White-only universities, and acts that repealed Black South African citizenship. Unbelievably, Black South Africans could no longer hold passports.

During this era, the establishment's attitude toward Coloureds was somewhat indecisive. They were allotted limited rights, held a slightly more advantageous economic position than Blacks, but were not privy to the benefits accorded to Whites. The country's small Asian community was often ignored.

Apartheid was often classified as either "grand apartheid" or "petty apartheid." Grand apartheid focused on the partitioning of South Africa into separate states, while "petty" referred to the notion of segregation in general. The National Party, focused on grand apartheid, forced the evacuation of hundreds of thousands of people from their land—some say as many as 3.5 million people, including about 40,000 Whites. The Whites, however, were moved into desirable neighborhoods.

One new zone created for Blacks was Soweto, an acronym for South Western Townships. An estimated 60,000 Blacks were relocated to Soweto from Johannesburg, a largely black city. In 1955, one of the last refuges for Blacks in Johannesburg was Sophiatown. In the early hours of February 9, 1955, armed police forced the evacuation of the entire town despite the negative international attention the act was sure to draw. Residents were moved about nineteen kilometers (13 miles) away to Meadowlands. To the horror of Sophiatown residents, their homes were razed to make way for a new White suburb, Triomf (Triumph).

At the notorious Sharpeville massacre, on March 21, 1960, between 5,000 and 7,000 people had turned themselves in for not carrying their identity passbooks. A protest began, with fewer than twenty police officers present. By early afternoon, the police had set up armored vehicles facing the protesters. They opened fire. Officially, sixty-nine people were killed and over 180 injured. The response of the Black population was immediate: demonstrations, protest marches, strikes, and riots ensued, and nine days later a state of emergency was declared. More than 18,000 people were detained.

The Sharpeville massacre was a turning point in history for the South African government. A UN Security Council resolution expressed concern that the killing of unarmed protesters at Sharpeville constituted a threat to international stability and security. South Africa became increasingly isolated from the international community and slowly withdrew itself from the Commonwealth.

In early 1989, Frederik William de Klerk assumed the presidency of the National Party. He denounced apartheid, repealed discriminatory laws, ended the Land Act, and removed the ban on anti-apartheid political groups, including the African National Congress. Media restrictions were removed and political prisoners found not guilty of common-law crimes were released.

Anti-apartheid activist Nelson Mandela immediately set out to rally support for reconciliation and negotiations for a multi-racial South Africa. He prized cooperation and democracy. He was elected President in May 1994 and held office until 1999. On December 10, 1996, President Mandela chose Sharpeville as the site for the signing of the new Constitution of South Africa. In 1993, he was honored with the Nobel Peace Prize, which he shared with his supporter, former President de Klerk.

De Klerk retired from politics in 1997 and is recognized as an important leader for the end of apartheid. He served as Deputy President during Mandela's mandate and was the last White person to do so.

"I have fought against white domination, and I have fought against black domination. I have cherished the ideal of a democratic and free society in which all persons live together in harmony and with equal opportunities. It is an ideal which I hope to live for and to achieve. But if needs be, it is an ideal for which I am prepared to die."
—*Nelson Mandela, April 20, 1964*

Lower left: Children of Ekuvukene, which is a "resettlement" village in the Kwazulu "homeland," Natal. Millions of Black South Africans have been forcibly resettled in such villages since 1948, the largest forced movement of people in peacetime history.
Above: Nelson Mandela, Deputy President of the African National Congress of South Africa, addresses the Special Committee Against Apartheid in the General Assembly Hall on June 22 1990.

Human rights	10/10
Violence	8.5/10
World reach	4/10
Inevitability	9/10
Destruction	5/10
Average score	7.3/10

Patrick Bonneville: The Democratic Republic of Congo could be a paradise on earth. It is beautiful, has many resources, and is a haven for wildlife. In fact, DRC looks more like hell than paradise to its inhabitants. It is plagued by mass killings and rape. The concept of human rights does not seem to exist there. The country and its neighbors are among the most dangerous spots on earth today. The United Nations, the African Union, and, especially, DRC's neighbors cannot find solutions. The civilian population has been left to its fate.

The Democratic Republic of Congo is not to be confused with neighboring Republic of Congo. DRC borders with the Central African Republic, Sudan, Uganda, Rwanda, Burundi, Zambia, Angola, the Republic of the Congo, and Tanzania. Between 1971 and 1997, DRC was known as Zaire. Geographically, it is the third largest country in Africa and is located in the center of the continent. The Congo River runs through it and it has a forty-kilometer Atlantic Ocean coastline. According to the United Nations, DRC has an estimated population of 66 million people, making it the fourth most populous country in Africa, and the most populous French-speaking country in the world.

The country's recent history is more than turbulent. Having gained independence from Belgium in 1960, it almost immediately began experience growing pains. The First Congo War lasted about six months, from November 1996 to May 1997. Rebel leader Laurent-Désiré Kabila, backed by neighbors Uganda and Rwanda, overthrew Zairean President Mobutu Sésé Seko. Kabila declared himself president. The Second Congo War began on August 2, 1998. Although it officially ended in 2003, the country has not recovered and remains a volatile and hostile place today.

The Second Congo War directly involved eight African countries, making it the largest in African history. Also known as the Great War of Africa, about 5.4 million people died during and following the war. Millions of people not killed in battle or by disease and starvation were forced to flee to neighboring countries. Today, five years after the official end of the war, an estimated 1,000 people die daily from lingering effects, including preventable disease and malnutrition.

Opposite page: UN Volunteer human rights team in Bogoro investigates the 2003 Lendu militia crimes committed against civilians in the area.
Left: Thousands of civilians have fled their homes in Bunia in the Democratic Republic of the Congo while militia groups fight for control of the town. Looting is extensive.

Above: A casualty of fighting in Bunia, RDC.

Mobutu received backing from the USA, however the country found itself in chaos with four different leaders: Mobutu was in Leopoldville with the support of Western governments; Antoine Gizenga was in Stanleyville, supported by the Soviet Union and Egypt; Albert Kalonji was in South Kasai; and Moise Tshombe was in Katanga, supported by Belgian and Western mining interests.

Four years of struggle, murder, and abuses followed, until Mobutu managed to gain control over all regions of Zaire. Mobutu was an unforgiving and corrupt dictator. Although Zaire was rich with national resources, including copper, gold, and diamonds, the general population sank further into poverty. Mobutu, however, amassed a personal fortune estimated at $5 billion. As human rights abuse cases became public and corruption became evident, Belgium, France, and the USA all suspended military and financial assistance to the Zairean government.

Mobutu was forced into exile in 1997 and died a few months later in Morocco. Although elections have occurred and democratic rule is in place, there are several pockets of rebels who refuse to give up their power over certain regions. They cause much unrest for ethnic groups who fear persecution. President Joseph Kabila and Prime Minister Adolphe Muzito have survived three coup attempts. And while President Kabila is working toward building a war-free country, conflict continues to tear the DRC apart.

In the eastern regions of the country, Hutu and Tutsi forces fight to the death. Various militia groups battle for control over specific areas and block aid from entering their territory. Military groups extract minerals, diamonds, and timber to fund their war; they also impose exaggerated taxes on the people of the region and confiscate their livestock and food. In order to further their goals of ethnic cleansing and control of the country's natural resources, these groups have, tragically, embraced rape and sexual violence as a major means of warfare.

"The deaths caused to us by the Rwandans are indescribable and incalculable. We will repulse them, and this time round, we will pursue them into their territory and do to them what they did to us in our soil. You will detect enemies and massacre them without mercy."
—Congolese Major Mudenke, speaking on national radio, August 12, 1998

In the Eastern Congo, rape and other violent sexual abuse are considered the worst in the world. Amnesty International has reported that some 40,000 victims were raped between 1998 and 2004. Of course, this figures represents only those brave enough to seek treatment, and the actual figure must be estimated to be much higher. The prevalent practice of gang rape has contributed to an increase of cases of sexually transmitted diseases including HIV.

No ethnic group is safe. The pygmies, long believed to be the original inhabitants of Central Africa, are considered by both sides of this war to be subhuman. Les Effaceurs of North Kivu aim to rid the land completely of the pygmy population. Although all rebel groups are guilty of crimes against the pygmies, the Movement for the Liberation of Congo, a branch of the transitional government that controls the North, is widely believed to lead the violence and cannibalism.

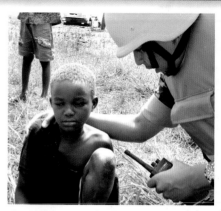

Above: The UN mission's headquarters was attacked in 2003. A UN blue helmet tries to comfort a young refugee.

"I am convinced now... that the lives of Congolese people no longer mean anything to anybody. Not to those who kill us like flies, our brothers who help kill us or those you call the international community... Even God does not listen to our prayers any more and abandons us."
—*Salvatore Bulamuzi, member of the Lendu community, who lost his family in northeastern DRC*

"Congo is the deadliest crisis anywhere in the world over the past 60 years. Ignorance about its scale and impact is almost universal and international engagement remains completely out of proportion to humanitarian need."
—*Richard Brennan, health director of the New York-based International Rescue Committee, 2006*

Human rights	10/10
Violence	10/10
World reach	3/10
Inevitability	6/10
Destruction	7.5/10
Average score	7.3/10

"*My colleagues, every statement I make today is backed up by sources, solid sources. These are not assertions. What we're giving you are facts and conclusions based on solid intelligence.*"
—Colin Powell, United Nations Security Council, February 5, 2003

Patrick Bonneville: Before the war, Iraq was a dictatorship run by Saddam Hussein. Iraq had invaded its neighbor, Kuwait, 10 years earlier, and it had used chemical weapons against one of its own minority peoples, the Kurds. As a result, Iraq was under massive international embargos. These embargos made life harsh for Iraqis. Nevertheless, according to the United Nations, the country was pretty much under control. Then George W. Bush decided that invading Iraq was necessary for world security, and especially for the security of the United States. The USA passed over the United Nations and declared war against Saddam Hussein based on a flimsy possibility that the country illicitly held weapons of mass destruction.

The invasion of Iraq divided the United States and it divided the world, especially amongst Western countries. While the United Kingdom joined the United States hand in hand in their endeavor, Canada, Germany, and France stepped aside, preferring to work with the United Nations.

On March 20, 2003, the United States, under President George W. Bush, launched an invasion of Iraq. Supported also by the United Kingdom, the Iraq War continues today. The invasion was, allegedly, a response to evidence that Iraq possessed weapons of mass destruction (WMD) that threatened the West and Israel. In fact, the United Nations never found their own evidence of such weapons.

Numerous countries criticized the invasion: Canada, Belgium, Chile, Russia, France, the People's Republic of China, Germany, Switzerland, the Vatican, India, Indonesia, Malaysia, Brazil, Mexico, the Arab League, the African Union, and many others. Although these and other countries publicly opposed the war, they were not manifestly in support of Saddam Hussein or his regime and none offered any assistance to Iraq.

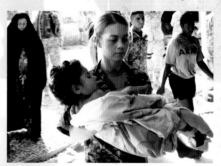

Opposite page: Protesters march towards the U.S. Capitol in Washington, DC, September 15, 2007.
Left: Iraqi woman with U.S. soldiers.
Above: According to the UNHCR, the war created 4.7 million refugees, more than 16% of the total Iraqi population.

The lead-up to the invasion is remarkable. In 2002, the United Nations returned to Iraq to investigate allegations of WMDs set out by the USA and a few other countries, including some who had actually shared weapons intelligence with Iraq in the 1980s. In December 2002, Iraq filed a 12,000-page weapons declaration with the UN. On December 19, U.S. Secretary of State, Colin Powell, stated that Iraq was in material breach of the Security Council resolution. They believed that the report did not account for all chemical and biological weapons. Colin Powell presented his arguments to the United Nations on February 5, 2003 and pushed for the UN to engage in war against Iraq. He also claimed that Iraq was harboring Abu Musab al-Zarqawi, an Al-Qaeda operative. The UN did not agree with the claims.

Because the USA could not secure support from the United Nations, it decided to attack without authorization. The U.S. Congress passed a joint resolution authorizing the Iraq War; the vote passed with 297 for and 133 against; only 6 of the 223 Republican representatives voted against the resolution.

"If UN inspectors need more time, they should be given more time. Why should we be in a hurry to wage war?"
—*Arab League Secretary General Amr Moussa, about the UN's inspections of weapons of mass destruction in Iraq, January 28, 2003*

Left: Over 100,000 Iraqi civilians have lost their homes since 2003.
Above: Stephen Colbert interviews Gen. Ray Odierno, Commanding General of the Multi-National Force-Iraq.

"I hope we do not see another Iraq-type operation for a long time— without UN approval and much broader support from the international community . . . I have indicated it was not in conformity with the UN charter from our point of view, from the charter point of view, it was illegal."
—*Former United Nations Secretary-General Kofi Annan, 2004*

Human rights	6/10
Violence	9/10
World reach	7/10
Inevitability	7.5/10
Destruction	7/10
Average score	7.3/10

"You are our brothers. I beseech your to not turn this country into a living hell. Will you not have to show your faces and confront your conscience some day? If we can peaceably settle our differences there is still hope that we can co-exist as brothers. Otherwise there is no hope. If you choose the other path, we may never come face one another again."
—Sheikh Mujibur Rahman, Bengali nationalist leader, addressing West Pakistan on March 7, 1971

"Our government has failed to denounce the suppression of democracy. Our government has failed to denounce atrocities. Our government has failed to take forceful measures to protect its citizens while at the same time bending over backwards to placate the West Pakistan dominated government."
—Archer Kent Blood, American diplomat, in a telegram, April 6, 1971

Patrick Bonneville: The Bangladesh Liberation War proved that rape is a powerful weapon of genocide. This war also taught us that humanity has learned few lessons from the Holocaust and World War II.

On March 26, 1971, the dominant West Pakistan went to war against East Pakistan and India. The result was the creation of Bangladesh out of the former East Pakistan. According to the Hamoodur Rahman Commission, 26,000 people were killed by Pakistan in the struggle to quash Bengali nationalism. According to Bangladesh, three million were killed.

The region was already broken: the Bangladesh Liberation War happened just one year after the devastating 1970 Bhola cyclone, which is believed to have claimed up to 500,000 lives. The region was slowly trying to recover from the killer storm, without any support or help from the national government; that help never came. Instead the groundwork was laid for conflict between a frustrated people and a heavily armed national Pakistani military.

Fourth months after the cyclone hit East Pakistan, the Pakistani army launched Operation Searchlight to break the Bengali nationalist movement and any hope of independence in the region. East Pakistan, or what was left of it, would remain the property of Pakistan, no matter how many lives the operation would cost.

Bengalis stood up to Pakistan, at a very high price. Civilians were tortured, raped, and murdered. Families were torn apart. The Dhaka University and its students were attacked. Bengali women and young girls were taken by the Pakistan Army as sex slaves. For Bengalis, the world had become a living hell.

On December 16, 1971, India compelled the Pakistani army to surrender. On March 26, 1971, Bangladesh declared itself independent from Pakistan; today, that date is marked by Bengalis as Independence Day.

Human rights	9/10
Violence	10/10
World reach	5/10
Inevitability	5/10
Destruction	7/10
Average score	7.2/10

Left: Bengali women and girls in particular suffered during the Bangladesh Liberation War. They were often raped and used as sex slaves.
Right: The Blood Telegram written by Archer Kent Blood, an American Consul General to Dhaka during the war. He warned the American authorities of the the atrocities committed in the Bangladesh Liberation War.

Department of State TELEGRAM

CONFIDENTIAL 084

PAGE 01   DACCA 01138   061008Z

21
ACTION NEA-08

INFO OCT-01   SS-20   AID-12   USIE-00   NSC-10   NSCE-00   CIAE-00

INR-07   SSO-00   RSR-01   RSC-01   /060 W

092431

P 060730Z APR 71
FM AMCONSUL DACCA
TO SECSTATE WASHDC PRIORITY 3124
AMEMBASSY ISLAMABAD
INFO AMCONSUL KARACHI
AMCONSUL LAHORE

C O N F I D E N T I A L DACCA 1138
LIMDIS
SUBJ: DISSENT FROM U.S. POLICY TOWARD EAST PAKISTAN:

JOINT STATE/AID/USIS MESSAGE

1. AWARE OF THE TASK FORCE PROPOSALS ON "OPENESS" IN
THE FOREIGN SERVICE, AND WITH THE CONVICTION THAT U.S.
POLICY RELATED TO RECENT DEVELORMENTS IN EAST PAKISTAN
SERVES NEITHER OUR MORAL INTERESTS BROADLY DEFINED NOR
OUR NATIONAL INTERESTS NARROWLY DEFINED, NUMEROUS OFFICERS
OF AMCONGEN DACCA, USAID DACCA AND USIS DACCA CONSIDER
IT THEIR DUTY TO REGISTER STRONG DISSENT WITH FUNDAMENTAL
ASPECTS OF THIS POLICY. OUR GOVERNMENT HAS FAILED TO
DENOUNCE THE SUPPRESSION OF DEMOCRACY. OUR GOVERNMENT
HAS FAILED TO DENOUNCE ATROCITIES. OUR GOVERNMENT HAS
FAILED TO TAKE FORCEFUL MEASURES TO PROTECT ITS CITIZENS
WHILE AT THE SAME TIME BENDING OVER BACKWARDS TO PLACATE
THE WEST PAK DOMINATED GOVERNMENT AND TO LESSEN LIKELY
AND DESERVEDLY NEGATIVE INTERNATIONAL PUBLIC RELATIONS
IMPACT AGAINST THEM. OUR GOVERNMENT HAS EVIDENCED WHAT
MANY WILL CONSIDER MORAL BANKRUPTCY, IRONICALLY AT A
TIME WHEN THE USSR SENT PRESIDENT YAHYA A MESSAGE DEFEND-
ING DEMOCRACY, COMDEMNING ARREST OF LEADER OF DEMOCRATI-
CALLY ELECTED MAJORITY PARTY (INCIDENTALLY PRO-WEST) AND
CALLING FOR END TO REPRESSIVE MEASURES AND BLOODSHED.
IN OUR MOST RECENT POLICY PAPER FOR PAKISTAN, OUR IN-
TERESTS IN PAKISTAN WERE DEFINED AS PRIMARILY HUMANI-

CONFIDENTIAL

Patrick Bonneville: This war, which took place in the early 1950's, got lost in the shadow of World War II.

In 1950, World War II was over, and the Korean peninsula had been freed from the Japanese empire. The United States and the Soviet Union, two allies in the war, decided to divide the region along the thirty-eighth parallel, creating the Republic of Korea and the Democratic People's Republic of Korea. The two countries were hoping for the best when they made the division but it soon turned out to be a fiasco. On June 25, 1950, communist North Korea invaded South Korea. It was the first step toward the Cold War.

The response by the United States and the international community was swift and powerful. The United Nations engaged in Korea on September 1950: eighteen nations arrived to fight against North Korea, which was supported by China and the Soviet Union. Over 1,200,000 people fought for each side.

The civilian populations of both countries were devastated. South Korea lost nearly 374,000 civilians and 138,000 soldiers in the war. It is estimated that over 1,500,000 civilians were killed or wounded. The United States lost 36,516 soldiers to the action. China is believed to have lost about 400,000. These casualties were doubly significant, since the world had just begun to make its way out of the heavy military and civil losses of World War II. India proposed the Korean War armistice to the United Nations in 1953, which was accepted by UN member nations. The United Nations Command ceased fire on July, 27, 1953, near the thirty-eighth parallel, and the Korean Demilitarized Zone was established.

Many war crimes were committed. The North Korean army assassinated academic, political, and religious leaders who might lead resistance from the North. In the South, pro-North political prisoners were executed and buried in mass graves. Families were separated, and the armies of both countries forcibly conscripted civilians to their ranks. American soldiers were ordered to "shoot first and ask questions later" for a period during the war, when that army chose to believe that civilians posed a threat to their military actions.

Human rights	8/10
Violence	8/10
World reach	7/10
Inevitability	6/10
Destruction	7/10
Average score	7.2/10

Upper left: Korean War Memorial in Washington.
Right: Korean War Memorial in Seoul.

"Mr. President, I have very serious news. The North Koreans have invaded South Korea."
—U.S. Secretary of State Dean Acheson to American President Harry S. Truman

*Patrick Bonneville: Afghanistan: a
country that does not know peace. It is
a country defined by war, both past and
present. Alexander the Great fought in
Afghanistan, as did the Arabs, Mon-
gols, British, and then the Russians.
Now, Americans, Canadians, and their
allies are involved. Will this region ever
know peace? Will it ever be at rest?*

The Great Game

In this historical antagonism that
sets the stage for the present conflicts,
the British Empire and the Russian Empire vied for control of Central Asia. The
Great Game was their struggle over this
stretch of land some 2,000 miles wide.
Cities virtually unknown to Western-
ers at the start of the nineteenth century
were at the heart of this battle for control. The British Empire was determined
to control the area, partly in an effort to
keep control over trade routes leading
to India and partly to stop the Soviet
Union's desire to expand.

The Great Game lasted roughly 100
years, beginning in 1813, at the onset of
the Russo-Persian Treaty, and ending in
1907 with the Anglo-Russian Convention. A second period of the Great Game,
albeit much less intense, began in 1917
with the Bolshevik Revolution. Later, in
the early 1920s, Afghanistan signed the
Treaty of Friendship with the Russian
Soviet Republic after having received
endowments of cash, technology, and
military equipment. Afghanistan, nevertheless, did not relinquish control to the
Soviet Union. World War II created

new problems, new allegiances, and new
conflicts. Britain and the Soviet Union
formed a brief alliance and exerted enormous pressure on Afghanistan to evict
the German contingent stationed there.
This allegiance ended the Great Game.

Soviet war in Afghanistan

In the second half of the twentieth
century, the situation in Afghanistan
changed. The pro-Soviet Democratic
Republic of Afghanistan was opposed by a group of loosely affiliated
Mujahideen, or "freedom fighters."
The Soviet-Afghan War was an attempt by the Soviets to control the the
Mujahideen resistance—purportedly
supported by the USA, Saudi Arabia,
and Pakistan—through an alliance with
the Marxist People's Democratic Party
of Afghanistan (PDPA). In essence, the
Soviet Union invaded Afghanistan to
ensure the continuation of communism
in that country.

The Soviet operation in Afghanistan began on Christmas Eve, 1979, and Soviet
forces withdrew in May 1988. This nine-
year stretch was scarred by executions,
forced confinement, forced occupation,
guerrilla warfare, and over one million
Afghan deaths. Of the 620,000 Soviet
soldiers involved in the war, close to
15,000 were killed; of those who survived, a staggering 92 percent were left
disabled. The war is often compared to
the American invasion of Vietnam.

Right: Opium poppy. Afghanistan is, as of March
2008, the greatest illicit opium producer in the
world. The industry contributes largely to the
country's instability.

"The social costs of two decades of civil war in Afghanistan have been enormous. More than one million civilians are believed to have been killed and countless others injured. During the time of the Soviet occupation, over six million people fled the country. Although many returned after the Soviet withdrawal, there are still over two million Afghan refugees in Iran and Pakistan, making Afghans the largest single refugee group in the world."
—Amnesty International

Human rights	7.5/10
Violence	9/10
World reach	7/10
Inevitability	5/10
Destruction	8.5/10
Average score	7.4/10

Afghan Civil War

The withdrawal of the Soviet Union was the catapult for the civil war. The Democratic Republic of Afghanistan was left to its own resources in defending itself against the Mujahideen. The government struggled for nearly four difficult years and finally fell in 1992. This opened the door for a relatively new group to appear on the scene: the Taliban.

Explanations of the origins of the Taliban vary. One account claims they formed from a group of devote Pashtan fundamentalist Sunni Muslims who had witnessed members of the Mujahideen rape and murder a family's children. They then organized with the mission to drive the Mujahideen out of Afghanistan once and for all. The second account claims that a trade organization from Pakistan recruited and trained the fundamentalists to clear trade routes into Afghanistan.

As they began to rise to power, the Taliban became popular among the general population because of their relentlessness in driving out the Mujahideen. By 1994, they had gathered enough support to capture the city of Kandahar and from there, expansion was inevitable. In 1996, the Taliban declared their country the Islamic Emirate of Afghanistan. Pakistan recognized the Taliban as the legitimate rulers of the country. By the year 2000, the Taliban controlled 95 percent of the region. Four years into their rule, however, their original mission had been discarded and they assumed the role of policing and governing according to Sharia law.

On September 11, 2001, the radical Islamic group Al-Qaeda launched a suicide terrorist attack on the United States. Thousands of civilians were killed as three passenger jets crashed into buildings in New York and Washington, and a fourth was crashed to the ground in Pennsylvania. The reaction of the American public and government in the following days and weeks was of anger and fear. It was at this moment that NATO joined the fight against terrorism.

It was believed that the Taliban were harbouring Al-Qaeda. In October 2001, the United States partnered with the United Kingdom to launch Operation Enduring Freedom in Afghanistan. Additionally, a NATO-led initiative called the International Security Assistance Force was authorized to "fight the war on terror" in that country. The aim was to find, charge, try, and convict Osama bin Laden and other high-ranking Al-Qaeda members. The end goal was to completely destroy all traces of Al-Qaeda and the Taliban regime. The U.S. created the "Bush Doctrine," which stipulated that governments and organizations sympathetic to the Taliban would be considered terrorists.

Today, eight years into the initiative, the situation in Afghanistan is far from resolved. It is unclear to most observers whether the NATO military presence resonates with suitable purpose.

Left: NATO has sent 90,000 troops to Afghanistan since December 2001, more than half of them American soldiers.

Officially called the Democratic Republic of Timor-Leste, East Timor is a short flight northwest of Darwin, Australia, in Southeast Asia. Neighboring Indonesia occupied the country from December 1975 to October 1999 in a quarter century of torture, starvation, executions, and other human rights abuses.

Portugal colonized East Timor in the sixteenth century and ruled the nation for hundreds of years. In 1974, a coup in Portugal forced the government to pull out of all its colonies. East Timor found itself in a situation of sudden independence. The Fretilin pro-independent organization declared victory in a small civil war and established government in the capital city of Dili. It was a short-lived government, for on December 7, 1979, the Indonesian military stormed the country and destroyed any resistance. Firmly planted, they declared East Timor a province of Indonesia.

The 1991 Santa Cruz Massacre shocked the international community. The slaughter occurred following a relatively quiet demonstration by pro-independence supporters. The crowd had gathered to march to the cemetery for the funeral of Sebastiao Gomes, a known pro-independence supporter who had been killed earlier that week. Several journalists were in the country for a special visit by the UN Special Rapporteur for Human Rights; they secretly filmed the killing of 200 protesters. The international community

Above: 1998 manifestation in Timor-Leste.
Right: Mirko Fernandez, forensic anthropologist of the United Nations in Timor-Leste.

was quick to respond, and the event became an embarrassment for Indonesia. The USA withdrew its funding of the Indonesian military and eventually withdrew arms sales as well.

In 1996, East Timor independence fighters Carlos Filipe Ximenes Belo and José Ramos-Horta were awarded the Nobel Peace Prize for their efforts to bring stability and peace to their country. In 1999, the country went to the polls and an overwhelming majority voted for independence. After the 1999 vote, another wave of violence swept the nation. The United Nations set up a transitional administration and a Serious Crimes Unit. It is estimated that some 500,000 people were displaced during the months that followed the 1999 vote and that the Indonesian occupation claimed the lives of more than 100,000 East Timorese. In 2002, East Timor finally received its independence.

"I'm very concerned about what's happened in East Timor. We have ignored it so far in ways that I think are unconscionable."
—*President Bill Clinton*

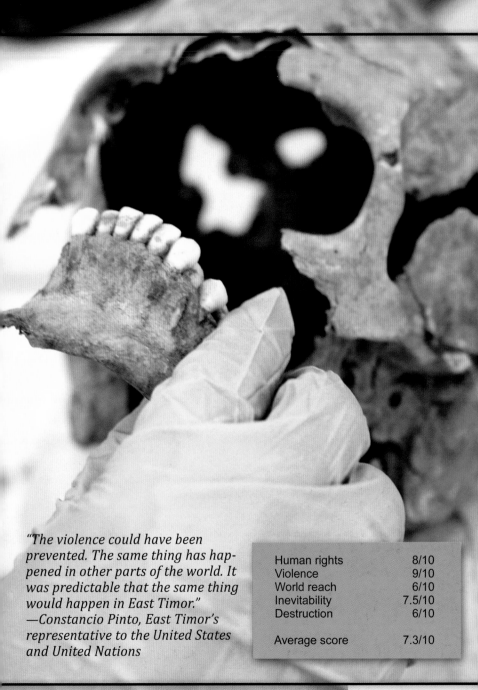

"The violence could have been prevented. The same thing has happened in other parts of the world. It was predictable that the same thing would happen in East Timor."
—Constancio Pinto, East Timor's representative to the United States and United Nations

Human rights	8/10
Violence	9/10
World reach	6/10
Inevitability	7.5/10
Destruction	6/10
Average score	7.3/10

Above: An Iranian command and control platform after shelling from four US Navy destroyers during Operation Nimble Archer. The shelling was a response to a recent Iranian missile attack on a reflagged Kuwaiti supertanker.
Right: Iraqi Air Force Mirage F-1EQ pilots prepare for an attack on Iranian targets.

The Iran–Iraq War was an armed conflict between Iraq and Iran that lasted from September 1980 to August 1988. Iraq's Saddam Hussein and Iran's Ayatollah Khomeini spearheaded the war.

In September 22, 1980, Iran was in the midst of a revolution. Iraq saw a chance to attack a weakened neighbor and invaded under the guise of a long-standing border dispute. In fact, there was a deeper and more immediate reason: Iraq's Saddam Hussein feared that his own carefully suppressed Shia population would agitate and rise up in response to Iran's politico-religious revolution. Iraq could invade Iran, suppress the Shia, gain important territory, and become the most influential nation in the Persian Gulf region.

Hussein and Khomeini really only accomplished two things during this dispute: the deaths of hundreds of thousands of soldiers and civilians on both sides of the border (which, in the end, did not change) as well important

economic damage to both nations. Hussein and his country's attempt at domination meant that they were on the offensive during the course of the conflict. In the meantime, Khomeini urged Muslims everywhere to rise up and create a unified mega-Islamic power.

When it became evident that Iran was not as weak as previously thought, Iraq reverted to chemical weapons.

In 1987, Iran's Khomeini attacked Kuwaiti oil tankers in the Persian Gulf, prompting the involvement of the United States and several Western European nations. Khomeini was no longer able to obtain arms. This forced the country to accept a ceasefire by the United Nations in 1988.

During the conflict, Iran obtained support or arms from Syria, Libya, North Korea and China. Iraq was supported by some Arab and Western countries as well as by the Soviet Union, which supplied many of their arms. Iraq withdrew troops from Iran in 1990. The last of both countries' prisoners of war were only released in 2003.

Human rights	9/10
Violence	9/10
World reach	5/10
Inevitability	5/10
Destruction	8/10
Average score	7.2/10

The Ottoman Empire, ruled from Constantinople, lasted from 1299 to 1922, when it was succeeded by the Republic of Turkey. The Ottoman Empire entered World War I on the side of the German Empire and the Kingdom of Bulgaria; collectively, they were the Central Powers. When they were unsuccessful in their attempts to overtake certain regions, they blamed their failure on the Armenian population.

Armenia was a landlocked province to the east of Turkey that bordered, at the time, the Russian Empire and the Persian Empire. The Ottoman government became hostile to its Armenian population when volunteers from that region worked in aid of the Russian army in their advances into Armenian territory. The hostility was so great that it led to a policy of genocide—a clear will to completely eliminate the Armenian population. Around April 24, 1915, 250 Armenian intellectuals and leaders in Constantinople were arrested. Armenian families were evicted from their homes and massacred or sent on death marches, forced to march hundreds of miles to what is now Syria, without food, water, or shelter. Women and children were repeatedly raped and death was virtually inevitable. Some scholars estimate that as many as two million Armenians and other minor ethnic groups in the region were killed between 1915 and 1923. About 500,000 fled to neighboring countries.

France, Russia, and Great Britain publicly deplored the acts of the Ottoman government, defining them as a "new crime against humanity and civilization." In 1943, the expression "genocide" was coined to describe the wilful extermination of the Armenian people. Today, the Republic of Turkey, which succeeded the Ottoman Empire, refuses to acknowledge their actions as genocidal.

"Who, after all, speaks today of the annihilation of the Armenians?"
—Adolf Hitler, while persuading his associates that a Jewish holocaust would be tolerated by the West, August 22, 1939

Human rights	10/10
Violence	10/10
World reach	2/10
Inevitability	8/10
Destruction	6/10
Average score	7.2/10

Left and right: Remembering the victims. Over 135 memorials, spread across 25 countries, commemorate the Armenian genocide.

"I screamed, but there was no one left to hear me."
—Aras Abed, survivor

In March 1988, the Iraqi government launched a gas attack against the inhabitants of the Kurdish town Halabja. As many as 5,000 people were reported killed immediately upon the attack, and another 10,000 were injured. In the months and years since, thousands more deaths and birth defects have been attributed to the gas attack. Human Rights Watch declared the attack to be one of genocide and the largest chemical weapons attack against a civilian population.

The two-day attack involved several chemical agents, including mustard gas and the nerve agents sarin, soman, tabun, and VX. Some people just dropped dead, others died slowly, from toxic burns or blisters. Witnesses reported gases that "caused things to catch fire." People who touched another's burns would begin to burn themselves.

Reports described a scene like something from a horror movie. The effects of the various gases worsened with time, and those who died while trying to leave the city were left where they fell. Parents had to abandon their already dead children. Some witnesses say as many as 6,000 fled to the bordering mountains, risking even further injury or death from landmines.

Some civilians made it to the border of Iran where doctors and military personnel were standing by to help. For some, the help was too late, but the remainder were sent to refugee camps until it was safe to go home. But Iraq left no houses

Above: Every single life was terminated that day.

standing; Halabja was flattened with dynamite and bulldozers. So, too, was the nearby town of Sayed Sadeq. Almost every Kurdish village in northern Iraq— an estimated 4,000—was attacked or destroyed. About one million Kurdish people were displaced, and there were up to 150,000 deaths. Countless numbers of widows and orphans were left.

Ali Hassan Abd al-Majid al-Tikritieh, a cousin of former President Saddam Hussein, was found to be responsible for the attacks against the Kurds.

"Some villagers came to our chopper. They had 15 or 16 beautiful children, begging us to take them to hospital. So all the press sat there and we were each handed a child to carry. As we took off, fluid came out of my little girl's mouth and she died in my arms."
—Kaveh Golestan, photographer

Human rights	10/10
Violence	10/10
World reach	2/10
Inevitability	8/10
Destruction	6/10
Average score	7.2/10

SOMALI
PIRATE

"In 2008, the number of reported piracy attacks off East Africa rose astronomically. Barely a day seemed to pass without a new incident being reported."
—International Maritime Organization

Patrick Bonneville: Only one word can describe Somalia: anarchy.

Somalia is a Muslim country located in the Horn of Africa with a population that surpasses nine million people. It was an important trade route in the ancient world. Somalia had successfully kept the great colonizer, the British Empire, at bay for decades, until the 1929 British bombardment forced it into the Empire. Somalia gained independence from the UK in 1960.

Thanks to its close ties to Arab nations, it was accepted as a member of the Arab League in 1974. Somalia also joined the African union and supported the African National Congress in South Africa. Although it has a free market economy, the country has suffered from the instability of civil wars.

After unsuccessful attempts at diplomacy, in 1977 Somalia invaded Ethiopia with a plan to recapture Somali lands that had been partitioned by former powers. The government was eager to establish self-determination for the ethnic Somalis living in these territories. The move drew criticism from certain countries, such as the Soviet Union. Others, such as the USA and Egypt, sided with Somalia and provided weapons, money, and military training. Somalia's Ogaden National Liberation Front (ONLF) appeared to be winning the war. However, with Ethiopia's backing from the Soviet Union and Cuba, Somalia found itself in a weakened position and by the following year, the war collapsed.

As the general population grew disillusioned with the Somali government, it seemed inevitable that the country would embark on a civil war. In 1991, forces backed by Ethiopia's ousted president Barre, and President Ali Mahdi Muhammad was selected as interim head of state. The northern portion of the country declared independence and adopted the name Somaliland that same year. This declaration has not been recognized by any foreign government. President Muhammad was not recognized by several factions, splitting the country further. Many territories within the country have claimed independence.

The civil war disrupted everyday life, from farming and agriculture to food distribution. Ethiopia stepped up its presence in 2006 and in June 2009, Somalia was forced to request aid from neighboring East African countries. Although the UN Security Council has been involved over the course of the war, they eventually withdrew in 1995, having suffered too many casualties.

Somalia has also gained international notoriety for its pirates, which have been a threat to off-shore international shipping since the beginning of its civil war. Because of the disorganization of the Somali government, there is little impetus to rein in the pirates. Worse, a lack of maritime regulation along the country's shores means that overfishing has become an important problem, and Asian and European companies dump toxic waste in waters near the coast.

Right: A Somali mother waits for food at a UNICEF Relief feeding centre in Mogadishu in 1992.

"Currently only about 19.9% per cent of Somali children are in school."
—UNICEF, 2005

Human rights	9/10
Violence	10/10
World reach	3/10
Inevitability	6/10
Destruction	8/10
Average score	7.2/10

Patrick Bonneville: The regions where the slave industry flourished are still not at peace. Liberia, Sierra Leone, Côte d'Ivoire: All these names evoke horrific atrocities: mass killings, warlords, weapons, and massacres. Is there a small seed of peace in the region? Is there some hope that the people living here can hang to? Can we wish for all these scars to heal and stay healed?

Sierra Leone

The Sierra Leone Civil War began in 1991 and ended in 2002. During this eleven-year war, the country spiralled into painful and devastating chaos. Tens of thousands of Sierra Leonians died, over two million were displaced, millions were mutilated or raped as a tactic of war, and thousands of children were forced into military service. Neighboring countries were obligated to shoulder the responsibility of thousands of refugees.

Control over the diamond industry is considered the chief catalyst of the war. Although Sierra Leone is rich in natural resources, the citizens are among the absolute poorest of the world. The Revolutionary United Front (RUF), under leader Foday Sankoh, began as a group of students who received secret military training from Moammar Qaddafi's Ghana and Libya training camps. The students spread the notion of revolution among the workers in the diamond mines.

Neighboring Liberia played an important financial role in the RUF. As the party tried to destabilize Sierra Leone and capture the all-important financial benefits of its resources, Liberian President Charles Taylor was active in sponsoring them. It is said that he helped develop a deal with the government on behalf of the RUF, whose platform seemed to include no ideology—they were neither culturally nor politically based.

The civil war was declared over in 2002, following the victory of President Kabbah and the SLPP party. The RUF party failed to win a single seat. Living conditions in Sierra Leone have changed little. It remains the lowest ranked country on the Human Development Index and is seventh-to-last on the Human Poverty Index. Its people are subject to corruption and misinformation, as there is no free press. Sierra Leone also has low literacy rates despite being home to the oldest university in western Africa.

"They told us to lie down in the road, face down. They had their guns to our heads. The first to be cut was Brima; they cut his left hand with an axe. Then my left hand was hacked off and then Amara's right hand. They didn't ask us any questions or accuse of us anything."
—Lansana, age twenty-four, victim of the rebels in Sierra Leone

Right: 10,000 child soldiers participated in Sierra Leone's civil war.

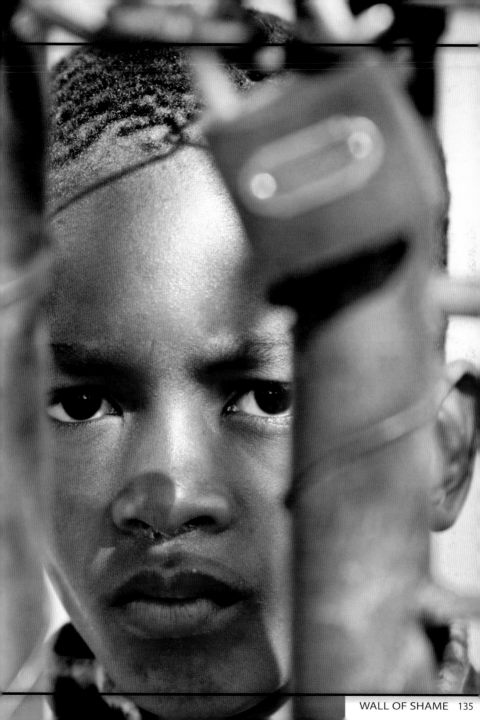

The current President, Ernest Bai Koroma of the All People's Congress, won a tight election in 2007. His presidency is focused on rebuilding the country into a truly democratic state, eliminating corruption and drug trade, and prosecuting those responsible for war crimes during the Sierra Leone Civil War.

Liberia First Civil War

The history of Liberia is unique among African nations, due to its roots as a colony founded by freed slaves from the United States. These freed slaves formed an elite group in Liberian society, and, in 1847, they formed a government based on that of the United States, naming their capital city, Monrovia, after James Monroe, the fifth president of the United States. This government was overthrown by a military-led coup in 1980, which marked the beginning of a period of instability and civil war that left hundreds of thousands of people dead and devastated the country's economy.

The coup of 1980 set the stage for Samuel Doe to rise to the presidency. His politics, however, were unpopular with the international community and eventually his party was drawn into civil conflict. His colleague Charles Taylor had created a rebel force known as the National Patriotic Front of Liberia (NPFL). The NPFL rebelled in 1989 in the most violent of manners, attacking innocent and unarmed civilians and burning entire villages.

Right: A homeless orphan of the Sierra Leone war sits on a pile of rubbish at the ferry port in Lungi, while United Nations peacekeepers awaits the ferry to the airport, at the end of tour of duty.

By the mid 1990s, the country was under the control of the NPFL. Doe was eventually captured, tortured, and killed. Peace was still far off, however. This civil war caused the deaths of over 200,000 Liberians. Children soldiers committed war crimes that seem unthinkable. The NPFL was responsible for the rape and murder of many people, regardless of age. Masses of Liberians were forced to flee their country, and the economic stability of Liberia was seemingly irreversibly compromised.

Liberia Second Civil War

1999, Liberia fell into civil war again. A Liberian rebel group attacked neighboring Guinea, leading to a two-year war with not only Guinea but Sierra Leone as well. The Guinea Republic and Sierra Leone supported the Liberians United for Reconciliation and Democracy (LURD) party, while the NPFL was still fighting for total control.

In this most complicated of wars, it seemed as though dozens of parties had sprung up everywhere, with manifestos of control or of democracy. In 2003, the Movement for Democracy in Liberia (MODEL) emerged in southern Liberia. The NPFL then controlled only one third of the country. Around this time, the USA sent troops to the area and Nigeria sent in peacekeepers. The capital city, Monrovia, was bombarded by LURD, leaving many thousands dead.

The bloody mess ended with the resignation of President Taylor, who negotiated the Accra Comprehensive Peace Agreement to end the war. He was subsequently flown into exile in Nigeria, which has refused to deport him to face charges of war crimes in

Sierra Leone. Vice-President Moses Blah was installed as President in 2003, however 80 percent of the country was still under rebel control. Today, Liberia is slowly recovering. Despite its poverty and lack of adequate infrastructure, it has experienced some economic growth. It remains today one of the poorest countries on Earth.

Côte d'Ivoire

The Ivorian Civil War began in 2002, when rebel troops stormed several cities, destroying anything in their path. Their goal was to gain control of the capital, Abidjan. Government forces were unable to repel the rebels, who gained valuable ground. As rebels threatened more attacks, France sent in troops in an effort to stop the sieges. While France claimed to be acting for the protection of French citizens in the region, their efforts aided the government. Their involvement remains controversial.

Although the civil war ended, theoretically, in late 2004, Côte d'Ivoire remains divided. United Nations peacekeepers face constant menace and are greatly outnumbered. A total of twenty-five UN personnel have been killed during their mission. It is hoped that the peace agreement signed in 2007 was truly the beginning of a new era for this torn nation.

"If the situation in Sierra Leone is so bad, how come there are 50,000 NATO troops in Kosovo and just a few dozen unarmed UN observers in Sierra Leone?"
— BBC correspondent Mark Doyle

Human rights	10/10
Violence	10/10
World reach	5/10
Inevitability	4.5/10
Destruction	6/10
Average score	7.1/10

Human rights	8/10
Violence	9.5/10
World reach	3/10
Inevitability	7/10
Destruction	7.5/10
Average score	7.0/10

From September 1, 1961 to May 29, 1991, war raged between Ethiopia and Eritrea, two of the poorest regions of the world. Thirty years of conflict and death ended in an almost unanimous agreement on the independence of Eritrea. Eritrea lost some 60,000 soldiers and 90,000 civilians in the conflict.

The war began with the shooting of Ethiopian army and police by an Eritrean man, Hamid Idris Awate, and his compatriots. The date was September 1, 1961. The 1961 shooting led to the annexation of Eritrea in 1962 by Emperor Haile Selassie of Ethiopia.

The Eritrean Liberation Front claimed that the dissolution of the Eritrean-Ethiopian federation violated the Eritrean federal constitution and denied the Eritrean people their right to self-determination. By this time, the movement claimed to be multi-ethnic, involving individuals from Eritrea's nine major ethnic groups.

In the mid-1970s, Eritrean rebel fighters united to form the Eritrean People's Liberation Front (EPLF), which would go on to lead a bitter civil war against Ethiopia. The leader of this umbrella organization was Secretary-General Ramadan Mohammed Nur. Much of the equipment used to combat Ethiopia was captured from its own army.

Left: Caskets of freedom fighters from Eritrea's war of seccession from Ethiopia, about to be buried at a patriot's cemetery in Massawa, 1992.

During this time, Ethiopia's Derg government could no longer control the population by force alone. Forces were sent on missions to instill fear in the population. In a terrible illustration of this strategy for control, on November 17, 1970, the entire village of Basik Dera in northern Eritrea was herded into the local mosque, whose doors were locked behind them. The building was then razed and the survivors were shot.

At the end of the 1980s, the Soviet Union informed Mengistu that it would not be renewing its defense and cooperation agreement. The capability of government forces in both regions collapsed as a result. Subsequently, Ethiopian government control of Eritrea was limited to the Keren-Asmera-Mitsiwa triangle and the port of Aseb to the southeast. The TPLF's victories in Tigray ultimately led to its total conquest by the rebels and the expansion of the insurgency into Gonder, Welo, and even parts of Shewa the following year.

After the Soviet withdrawal of support, the United States facilitated peace talks in Washington that eventually led to the fall of the Mengistu regime in May 1991. In mid-May, Mengistu resigned as head of the Ethiopian government and went into exile. The Ethiopian government recognized the right of Eritreans to hold a referendum on independence. In April 1993, the Eritrean people voted almost unanimously in favor of independence, a vote that was verified by the UN observer mission UNOVER.

Patrick Bonneville: Tibetans are not extremists. They do not seem to threaten the security of their neighbors. It is unlikely they have weapons of mass destruction. Their way of life seems to resonate with the whole world. They could have been such good partners for the Chinese central government. They are a tourism cash cow and a great partner for natural resources, including, of course, fresh water and hydro-electricity. Why, then, isolate them and force them to assimilate into Chinese culture? The outcome seems to be more negative than positive. Is there a tangible gain for the Chinese people?

Historically, Tibet has been a region of division. Unified under King Songtsän Gampo in the seventh century, it continued to expand through territorial advances into China and Nepal and through strategic marriages. Gampo is credited with bringing Buddhism to Tibet, where the religion grew. By the sixteenth century, the religious leader, the Dalai Lama, became the head of the region, not just the spiritual leader. During China's Qing Dynasty, from 1644-1912, Tibet was ruled as a Chinese dependency. In fact, only three of the fourteen Dalai Lamas have ever actually ruled Tibet. In 1913, the thirteenth Dalai Lama declared independence, a notion wholly rejected by China. The Chinese tightened their military presence in the region, eventually forcing Tenzin Gyatso, the current Dalai Lama, to seek asylum in India, where he remains to this day. Since the Chinese invasion of Tibet, in the 1950s, Tibetans live under the rule of the Communist Party of China, led by the Penchen Lama.

From 1913 to 1950, China was preoccupied with several civil wars and, of course, World War II. Tibet remained a quiet nation far from the worries of the Chinese government. They were not, however, off the radar. On October 7, 1950, the People's Liberation Army (PLA) defeated the Tibetan army in a battle at Chamdo. Although referred to as a "peaceful" operation, 5,000 Tibetan soldiers were killed. The People's Republic of China used this victory to declare sovereignty over Tibet. Representatives of the Dalai Lama signed the Seventeen Point Agreement, in which their defeat was acknowledged, however the Dalai Lama himself declared that it was "thrust upon the Tibetan government and people by the threat of arms."

The PRC proceeded to destroy the Tibetan culture. Of 2,500 monasteries, only 70 remain standing. An incredible 93 percent of monks were forced into exile, and, since 1950, 1.2 million people have died.

The UN General Assembly has condemned China for violating human rights in Tibet. Until Tibet can regain its independence, Tibetans remain under what can only be described as house arrest. There is no foreign media presence, no outside influence, only isolation.

Right: A young woman in London protests against the invasion of Tibet.

"The claim by the Dalai clique that the Chinese government is engaged in 'cultural genocide' in Tibet is nothing but a lie."
—Chinese Premier Wen Jiabao, March 2008

Human rights	9.5/10
Violence	7.5/10
World reach	3/10
Inevitability	9/10
Destruction	5.5/10
Average score	6.9/10

Laos's "secret war" began at the same time as the Vietnam War and lasted about twenty years. It was rooted in disagreement about the governmental structure that would reign in Vietnam. In 1961, North Vietnam advanced into South Vietnam, intent on establishing a communist government in Laos. The Pathet Lao, the communist Laotian party, allied with North Vietnam while the Royal Laotian party, the party in power, allied with the USA and Thailand. Thailand feared it would be the next target on the communist agenda if Laos failed to resist North Vietnam's advances.

This war between communist Vietnam and the American-Thai alliance mirrored the Vietnam War. In the end, Laos lost its fight against the communist regime. The USA withdrew, and the North Vietnamese presence continued in Laos. On December 2, 1975, the Laotian king was forced to abdicate his throne, and the new communist government wasted no time in taking complete control. They centralized operations and arrested any remaining members of the previous government and military and sent them to "re-education camps."

"This country used the Hmong. They trained them how to fight. Now the Hmong are dying because they were allies of the United States."
—Vaughn Vang, Lao human rights advocate

These actions led to the exodus of many ethnic Hmong people. About 10 percent of the population fled and sought refugee status in the USA, Thailand, and other neighboring nations.

Today, the country remains under a communist regime and rates consistently low on many humanitarian and economic indexes. The government heavily monitors media and there is very little freedom of the press. Several international media outlets have described the on-going torture and crimes carried out by the current communist regime.

In August 2009, U.S. Senator Jim Webb traveled to Laos on behalf of the Laotian community in the United States. His goal was to bring attention to and seek accountability for war crimes and crimes against humanity committed against Laotians; he and the people he represents wish to bring the criminals to justice at international courts in The Hague and restore democracy to their land.

Human rights	8/10
Violence	8/10
World reach	3/10
Inevitability	7/10
Destruction	8/10
Average score	6.8/10

Right: Laos is a field of landmines and cluster bombs. Over 13,000 people have been killed or maimed.

"When someone gave me the facts, they devastated me. I knew rape was a big problem in South Africa, but I had no idea how bad it was. One out of every three women there will be raped in her lifetime. Every 26 seconds, a woman is raped."
—South African actress and activist Charlize Theron

Patrick Bonneville: In South Africa, a country that has struggled for justice for its people, the rate of sexual assault surpasses all other regions of the world. According to the United Nations, South Africa has, by far, the highest amount of rapes per capita. Heartbreakingly, children and infants are also frequently raped, both because of the myth that having sex with a virgin cures AIDS and because of the tremendously violent circumstances in which South African men themselves are raised.

In the 1980s, there were about 16,000 rapes reported per year. In 2006, there were more than 55,000. It is estimated that only one in twenty rapes is actually reported, which means there might well be over 494,000 rapes per year in South Africa—1,300 per day, or one woman every seventeen seconds. This figure does not include children or infants.

According to Human Rights Watch, girls and women of all races and economic classes are victims of rape. Their perpetrators are classmates, teachers, family members, and strangers. Some traditional healers or "witch doctors" have mistakenly taught that having sex with a virgin can cleanse an HIV-positive man of the virus.

Right: President of South Africa Jacob Zuma was charged with rape in 2005, but the court decided it had been consensual sex. Verdict: not guilty.

"In South Africa you have a culture where men believe that they are sexually entitled to women. You don't get rape in a situation where you don't have massive gender inequalities. One of the key problems in this country is that people who commit rape don't think they are doing anything wrong."
—Dr Rachel Jewkes, a senior scientist with the South African Medical Research Council, in an interview with BBC, 2002

"It was 5 am on October 2, 2005, when I was woken up by a loud bang on my bedroom door. I got up to face a group of young men, some of whom I knew in the neighborhood. They asked me for my phone and money. As soon as I handed these to them, they dragged me out of the house and started raping me one after the other. I tried to make a dash for safety, but was caught by a second group."
—Buyisiwe, age twenty-nine

Human rights	10/10
Violence	10/10
World reach	3/10
Inevitability	8/10
Destruction	2/10
Average score	6.6/10

"2 bullets are produced for every man, woman and child on the planet each year."
—*Amnesty International*

Patrick Bonneville: In time of war, when bullets are shot, bombs dropped, and landmines planted, somebody somewhere is turning a profit. The arms industry is enormous. It is shocking to realize that seemingly peaceful countries such as Switzerland, Sweden, Belgium, Singapore, and the Netherlands are home to some of the biggest exporters of weapons.

Experts say that more than one trillion dollars is spent on military expenditures worldwide every year. In 2006, the combined sales of the world's 100 largest arms producing companies totaled $315 billion. In 2008, it is estimated that this dropped by half because of the credit crunch. The United States is the leading arms supplier, accounting for 36 percent of all sales. The US is followed by Russia, Britain, Germany, and China.

The Control Arms Campaign reported in 2003 that there are over 639 million small arms in circulation, and that over 1,135 companies based in more than 98 different countries manufacture small arms as well as their various components and ammunition. The Control Arms Campaign was founded by Amnesty International, Oxfam, and the International Action Network on Small Arms.

In 2008, there were sixteen major armed conflicts worldwide, two more than in 2007. According to the United Nations, small arms are the most often used in conflicts, repression, and crime, taking millions of lives each year. Small arms are relatively light and, tragically, are particularly suitable for child soldiers. There are an estimated 500 million small arms in circulation today worldwide.

The top three importers of arms are South Korea, India and Algeria. China is the fourth most important arms buyer. On the other hand, the United States and Russia are by far the biggest exporters, followed by Germany, France and the United Kingdom.

"When we see the thousands of young children bearing arms in today's conflicts, we have the right—indeed the duty—to react and attempt to change a situation where arms often seem to be more readily available than school books."
—Yves Sandoz, Director of International Law and Policy, International Committee of the Red Cross

"The only thing in abundance in Darfur is weapons. It's easier to get a Kalashnikov than a loaf of bread."
—Jan Egeland, UN Emergency Relief Coordinator, July 1, 2004

Human rights	1/10
Violence	4/10
World reach	10/10
Inevitability	9/10
Destruction	9/10
Average score	6.6/10

Human rights		9/10
Violence		9/10
World reach		2/10
Inevitability		7.5/10
Destruction		5.5/10
Average score		6.6/10

STOP
THE GENOCIDE
N SRILANKA

Patrick Bonneville: In July 23, 1983, a very dark passage in the history of humanity was written in Sri Lanka. The event would become known as Black July. Here, colonization has left a dark legacy that divides native peoples among themselves. The wound left by Black July does not seem to be healed yet. I hope it will.

Sri Lanka is an island nation off the southeast coast of India. The Tamils and Sinahlese peoples have called the island home for more than 25,000 years. It has been colonized by the Portuguese (1505-1658), the Dutch (1602-1796), and the British (from about 1815-1948). Historically, the Tamils occupied the northern tip of the island, while the Sinhalese were found throughout central and southern Sri Lanka. During the Portuguese and Dutch occupations, consideration for the different cultures and distinct societies was given.

With the arrival of the British, however, the two societies were merged for ease in management. Tamils were taught English and left farming for government and academic employment. By the time Sri Lanka gained independence from Britain, Tamils held a majority of the administrative positions even though they were a minority in the population. Over the next few decades, sporadic fighting and riots occurred as the Sinahlese population grew increasingly intolerant of the Tamils. In 1956, the government passed the controversial Sinhala Only Act that declared Sinahalese the only official language. Uproar from the Tamil community was met with violence.

In that clash, known as the Black July of 1983, angry mobs murdered, maimed, and burned Tamil people and their homes. Some estimates put the death toll at over 3,000. Sinhalese prisoners killed fifty-two Tamil political prisoners in Colombo's jail and a minibus full of Tamils was set on fire and the occupants left to burn to death. The event was witnessed by at least 100 bystanders, who were unable to help.

These deliberate acts of violence amount to genocide. They forced the exodus of over 150,000 Tamils. Australia and Canada were the first countries to offer refuge to survivors of the violence. Violence and discrimination against Tamils in Sri Lanka continues to this day. Their rights have been eliminated and their freedom is non-existent.

Tamil communities around the world gather on July 24 each year to remember the events of 1983.

"We lost every single thing in that riot except the clothes we were wearing. My mom, alone with 7 children, went through so many terrible problems after riots. In my family no one will forget this horrible racist and cruel incident."
—Sanjeevan Selladurai, survivor

Left: Tamil supporters demonstrate in Canada. Outside India, Sri Lanka and Malaysia, the most important Tamil communities are in Singapore, United Kingdom, Réunion and Canada.

On the twenty-eighth day of the second month of 1947 (hence the name "2-28"), a general uprising of the citizens of Taiwan against their government led to the violent murders of thousands of people. The 228 Massacre catapulted Taiwanese into the Kuomintang's "White Terror," during which thousands would die and thousands more would vanish. Because the Kuomintang (KMT) government hushed up the events, the actual death toll is unknown, although estimates range from ten to thirty thousand.

In 1895, Japan gained control over Taiwan as a result of the first Sino-Japanese war. At the end of World War II, however, Japan returned administrative control of Taiwan to the Republic of China. When China moved into Taiwan, hundreds of business owners lost control of their enterprises—the new Chinese government had the goal of monopolizing business. China effectively subjected the Taiwanese people to a dictatorship under the leadership of Governor-General Chen Yi.

The region fell into economic despair and ruin. Frustrations rose and anger mounted. Because of their Japanese-influenced culture, Taiwanese citizens were perceived as untrustworthy traitors by the new Chinese government. Hatred between the two cultures was rife. Tensions grew and by 1947, the entire nation was paralyzed with suspicion and anxiety about economic failure. A simple dispute between a female cigarette vendor and an officer of the Office of Monopoly led to the civil rebellion that kept Taiwan from international eyes for decades.

Forty-year old widow Lin Jiang-mai was selling contraband cigarettes in an effort to make a small living in a financially morbid Taiwan. One day, her stock of cigarettes, along with her life savings, were confiscated by agents of the government. One of them cracked her skull with his pistol. Outraged bystanders chased the agents, prompting police to shoot into the crowd haphazardly, killing bystander Chen Wen-xi.

The shooting was the straw that broke the camel's back. The following morning, the Governor-General's officers were ordered to fire with machine guns on unarmed demonstrators. Several protesters were killed. By March 4, the nation was under martial law with death as the penalty for disobedience. Curfews were enforced and leaders in the movement for Taiwan's independence or semi-independence groups were imprisoned. It is believed that Chen Yi's troops killed up to 4,000 people.

Right: The Flag of the Republic of China, which is now used to represent Taiwan. The blue represents nationalism and liberty. White represents democracy and equality. Red represents the people's livelihood and fraternity.

The event led to a long period of repression. Chen Yi was on a mission to re-educate the Taiwanese so that they would become Chinese. Thousands of Taiwanese and Chinese sympathizers were executed or imprisoned; many of them were wrongly accused.

This period of terror ended only in 1987. In 1995 the government offered a formal apology and today, February 28 is a national holiday in honor of the victims. A plaque marks the spot of the first shot that day, and many other memorials now dot Taiwan. The Chinese government has offered financial compensation to the families of victims, however few have come forward to make a claim—many people remain too afraid to step forward, preferring to forget rather than accept forgiveness. Also, even after so many years, the subject is a virtual taboo; most families do not discuss the period and often do not share with younger generations the names or even the fact that a member of their family was involved.

Formal requests to declassify government documents related to the time of terror have fallen on deaf ears. Some families of the massacre's victims are demanding that the government apprehend any living soldier involved in the violence and apply appropriate punishment. They are still waiting.

"An American who had just arrived in China from Taihoku said that troops from China arrived there on March 7 and indulged in three days of indiscriminate killing and looting. For a time everyone seen on the streets was shot at, homes were broken into and occupants killed. In the poorer sections the streets were said to have been littered with dead . . . There were instances of beheadings and mutilation of bodies, and women were raped . . ."
—The New York Times, March 29, 1947

Human rights	10/10
Violence	10/10
World reach	4/10
Inevitability	7/10
Destruction	2/10
Average score	6.6/10

Patrick Bonneville: This is one of the most cruel war tactics: surround your enemy, block all access, and let them starve to death—all of them, including innocent women and children. The Biafran famine was a spectacularly cowardly military action.

Between July 1967 and January 1970, the south-eastern provinces of Nigeria were inflamed by a movement for independence. Economic conditions were poor, and the Ibo people were defiant in proclaiming their own republic. Nigeria itself had gained independence from Britain in 1960, however the vast religious, linguistic, and ethnic differences within its borders created ripe conditions for civil war among its 60 million people.

The conflict truly began on May 30, 1967, when Chukwuemeka Odumegwu Ojukwu, the Eastern Region's military governor, announced the Republic of Biafra. Control of oil resources was a major issue during the conflict.

Initially, Biafra was strong and resisted the Nigerian advances on their claimed territory. In April of 1968, Nigeria initiated a new tactic to break the Biafran stronghold. They would close off the region from all sides; they created blockades on the northern fronts and captured Port Harcourt. It was not long before the blockade began to work. Widespread hunger overtook the Biafran population. Biafra declared itself a victim of genocide by Nigeria and sought international assistance. Aid organizations tried to send in medicine

Right: Biafran famine at its worst in 1968, captured by French doctor Patrick Valas.

and food but deliveries were delayed by the military.

A team of British doctors from the Liverpool University School of Tropical Medicine visited Biafra after the war, when they concluded that while starvation was evident, it was not clear to what extend the blockade had caused it. They considered the possibility that the Biafran military had kept food aid for themselves rather than distributing among the civilian population.

Both sides of the dispute claimed the other was responsible for the delay in aid delivery. Nigeria claimed that the Biafran government had hired foreign mercenaries in an effort to prolong the conflict. In turn, it is known that Nigeria had hired Egyptian pilots to fly their bomber and fighter jets to target, among others, Red Cross shelters. Red Cross volunteers were forced to sign gag orders so as not to reveal their knowledge of such events. One of the doctors on the ground during the famine, French doctor Bernard Kouchner, would later become cofounder of Médecins Sans Frontières in 1971.

The Nigerian government succeeded applying its will: after an estimated one million innocent people were killed through forced famine and starvation, Biafra was reabsorbed into Nigeria.

"...It (mass starvation) is a legitimate aspect of war..."
—Anthony Enahoro, Nigerian Commissioner for Information, July 1968

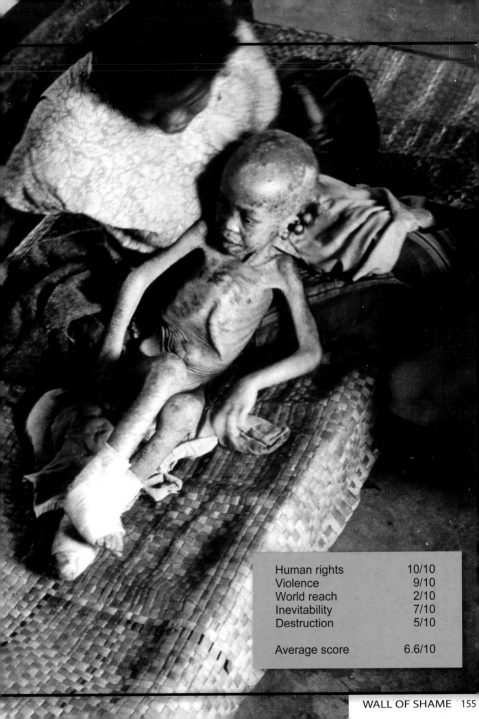

Human rights	10/10
Violence	9/10
World reach	2/10
Inevitability	7/10
Destruction	5/10
Average score	6.6/10

Left: One of the arms of choice in Ethiopia and in Africa, the AK-47 assault rifle.
Below: The country slowly returned to stability and a more normal life for its citizens in the 1990s.

Although they overlapped and affected each other, the Eritrean War of Independence and the Ethiopian Civil War were two separate events centered on different issues. Lasting from 1974 to 1991, the Ethiopian Civil War was the uprising of the population against the communist Derg junta. The Derg had come to power after a coup d'état against Emperor Haile Selassie's administration. The Derg, led by Marxist military leader Mengistu Haile Mariam, was financially supported by the Soviet Union and Cuba. This meant that Ethiopia was on its way to becoming a communist state. Rebel groups formed to oppose the regime. Somalia reinforced them, protecting its interests in the ethnic Somali region of Ethiopia.

Military fights between the junta and rebel groups went on for seventeen years. Some 250,000 people lost their lives, many of them because of their political opposition. In 1991, a coalition of rebels, with inside help from some of Mengistu's officials, took over the country. The United States intervened diplomatically to end the bloody fights, and Mengistu agreed to flee to Zimbabwe.

In 2006, Mengistu and seventy-two officials of the Derg were found guilty of genocide. Unfortunately, he was extradited to Ethiopia where he enjoys the protection of Zimbabwe's President Robert Mugabe.

"Members of the Derg who are present in court today and those who are being tried in absentia have conspired to destroy a political group and kill people with impunity."
—Judge Medhen Kiros in the trial against the Derg government for genocide and crimes against humanity

Human rights	8/10
Violence	9/10
World reach	2/10
Inevitability	8/10
Destruction	5.5/10
Average score	6.5/10

Patrick Bonneville: The day a coup d'état brought General Pinochet into power was a dark one for Chile and for human rights. In the 1970s and 1980s, thousands of Chileans fled their beloved country because of his reign of terror. Others, who stayed, were brutalized. His years of terror, dictatorship, and injustice have left deep wounds in Chileans' collective memory.

On September 11, 1973, President Salvador Allende, a democratically elected Marxist, was overthrown in a coup d'état by the army and its leader, General Augusto Pinochet. Allende's regime had enjoyed a close relationship with the Soviet Union, and while there is no evidence that the United States played a role in the rise of Pinochet, the USA's Nixon administration was pleased by the developments: Pinochet was seen, at first, as a new South American leader fighting against communism. His military dictatorship ruled the country from 1973 to 1990.

The first act of the military junta was to block any potential opposition. All left-wing parties in Chile were broken down and all potential left-wing leaders and partisans were crushed. In their efforts to quash any dream of rebellion, the Pinochet junta caused the "disappearance" of 2,279 people and tortured 32,000 others. Some 1,312 succeeded in fleeing the country.

One operation in particular terrorized the country and was a sign of the times to come: the *Caravana de la Muerte,* or "Caravan of Death," was an army squad that crossed the country by helicopter from south to north in October 1973 to execute ninety-seven people who were perceived as threats to the new regime. The dictatorship continued until 1980, when Pinochet saw himself elected as President of a new republic for an eight-year term. During this time, Chile progressed toward a free market economy, and became more permissive of trade unions, free speech, and free assembly. In 1988, Pinochet was not re-elected to the presidency and left Chile to settle in London, England.

His brutal past caught up with him, however, and he was arrested in the United Kingdom for human rights violations on October 10, 1998. He was returned to Chile to face charges against the crimes he committed there in the 1970s. He died before receiving his sentence.

Human rights	9/10
Violence	7/10
World reach	4/10
Inevitability	8/10
Destruction	4/10
Average score	6.4/10

In a little under a quarter of a century some 200,000 Algerians lost their lives in the Algerian Civil War, which began as an armed conflict between the government and a number of Islamist rebel groups. Although the war ended with the surrender of the Islamic Salvation Front (FIS) and the defeat of the Armed Islamic Group (GIA) in 2002, low-level fighting continues to this day.

Many groups were involved in the conflict. They included: the Islamic Salvation Front (FIS), the National Liberation Front (FLN), the Islamic Armed Movement (MIA), and the Armed Islamic Group (GIA). In late 1991, the FIS was gaining popularity and as a result, the FLN cancelled the country's elections. Then-President Chadli Bendjedid was removed from office and the military gained control. The FIS was subsequently banned and thousands of members were arrested. The people's reaction was to wage war against the government, under the influence of the Islamic Armed Movement (IAM), based in the mountains, and the Armed Islamic Group (GIA), based in cities and towns.

Attacks on the military and government soon became attacks on civilians. Both security forces and Islamists assassinated about seventy journalists. Ceasefire negotiations collapsed and fighting intensified over the following six years. Massacres peaked in 1997, around the parliamentary elections, which were won by the National Democratic Rally (RND).

In October 1988, massive demonstrations against the government occurred throughout the country. During "Black October," the army shot at and killed many demonstrators; some see the events as a prelude to the civil war that was waiting upon the doorstep.

After Black October, President Bendjedid decided a new constitution was in order, one that would be built on promises of "freedom of expression, association and assembly." It brought forth the possibility for the creation of new parties and groups—such as those involved in the civil war—and allowed for Islamic opinion.

In 1999, Abdelaziz Bouteflika was elected president and a new law was immediately passed which, for all practical purposes, gave amnesty to most guerrillas. A small sub-group of the GIA, the Salafist Group for Preaching and Combat (GSPC), continues active attacks on the military. The group hides in the eastern mountain ranges of Algeria and is the only known remaining group of the war still fighting.

"I don't understand; the army was surrounding Bentalha but they did not intervene. It's beyond comprehension. The massacre went on for several hours and then the terrorists left and no one stopped them."
—Survivor of the BentalhaMassacre

Right: UN Secretary-General Ban Ki-moon visits the site of the bomb blast that claimed the lives of 17 United Nations workers in Algiers.

Human rights	7.5/10
Violence	8/10
World reach	2.5/10
Inevitability	8/10
Destruction	6/10
Average score	6.4/10

"They separated the children and the girls of 15 to 20 years old. Then they began the massacre. First, they tortured the elderly, because they said the latter were guerrillas; then they threw two grenades and fired weapons. . . After executing the women, the men and the elderly, they took the children one by one, smashed them against the ground, and threw them into the flames. No one could escape because the Army had surrounded the entrance and exit of Plan de Sánchez, as well as the adjacent roads. . ."
- Survivor Benjamín Manuel Jerónimo, testifying at the Inter-American Commission On Human Rights

Kimberly Murray: Guatemala holds a special place in my heart. It was the first country outside Canada and the USA that I visited. It was the first time I left Western comfort behind and trekked into the wilds of a different language, different culture, and different reality. My memories are filled with smiling people, warm welcomes, and the laughter of children playing. Today I often wonder if they are still smiling and laughing or if the ravages of war have left them empty and without hope.

From 1960 to 1996, the people of Guatemala suffered through the longest civil war ever recorded in Latin America. In the battle between the government and insurgents, innocent lives were stolen and left scattered along the way.

The roots of the war go back to the mid-1940s, with the beginning of a movement to prevent communist takeover. The October Revolutionaries were left-wing liberal students and professionals led by Juan José Arévalo and later by Jacobo Arbez Guzmán. Over the course of the 1900s, the war passed through various phases of intensity, causing the murder of countless civilians. By the end of the civil war, an estimated 200,000 people were killed. The UN-sponsored Archbishop's Office for Human Rights released a report estimating that the Guatemalan army was responsible for 90 percent of the atrocities, and the insurgent guerrillas, less than 5 percent. An astounding 83 percent of the victims were Maya.

The war was also spurred by institutional discrimination against Guatemala's indigenous peoples, including the Maya. The insurgents were predominantly indigenous. European descendants controlled much of the land, and their persistent mistreatment of their fellow countrymen led to the creation of several guerrilla groups. These groups worked both independently and jointly to conduct economic sabotage and overthrow the government. In 1982, they combined forces and became the Guatemalan National Revolutionary Unity (URNG).

The insurgents were outnumbered from the beginning. They simply lacked the resources to overtake the army. The government did not feel much real threat from guerillas, whose regions they repressed politically and socially.

The military occupied a dominant position within the Guatemalan government and held absolute power for at least half a decade in the 1980s. Military control over state institutions was evident. The army was famous for its illegal prisons, in which suspects were interrogated, tortured, and degraded. Many prisoners "disappeared," apparently executed. These prisons were scattered around the country in army bases, police stations, and even in private homes.

Upper left: Government forces and state-sponsored paramilitaries were responsible for over 93% of the human rights violations during the war.
Left: One of the main reasons for the war was social discrimination against Guatemala's indigenous peoples, especialy against the Maya. This photo was taken during the war.

Human Rights Watch reported in 1984 on the massacre of 160 civilians in the village of Las Dos Erres. In 1982, the military forced their way into the town, and, according to the report, killed infants by slamming their heads against walls, repeatedly raped women over the course of the three-day siege, and buried some victims alive. It is believed that this was just one of over 400 massacres documented and labeled as acts of genocide. Fear of revenge from the military kept survivors quiet for years.

In 1996, the civil war ended in a fragile peace. It brutal history was outlined in a report released by the Commission for Historical Clarification of 1994. This commission was established through the Oslo Accord and its purpose was to conduct objective research and report on human rights violations and acts. They recorded 626 massacres, in which complete Mayan communities were exterminated, including cattle, crops, and homes. The aggression was not limited to paramilitary insurgents: children and women were killed in the most horrendous of manners, including being buried alive along side their murdered parents. Those who did not die, suffered.

Human rights	8/10
Violence	8/10
World reach	4/10
Inevitability	7/10
Destruction	5/10
Average score	6.4/10

Patrick Bonneville: When I dug a well in 2008 for my house, fresh, drinkable water gushed like an oil well. That day, I thought about Darfur's children.

There are three important resources in the world: gold, oil, and water. One is about riches. The second is about power. The third is about the most important thing of all—life. There have been wars based on water, which is used to irrigate crops, generate electricity, and hydrate human bodies and livestock. The UN Environmental Program has reported that there is a link between the conflict in Darfur and scarcity of water. And Libya seems to be draining all the water from under the Sahara—to the detriment of Chad.

Only two regions in the world have a greater supply of water than there is demand: northern regions of North America and southern regions of South America. And Russia is doing all right, thanks to Lake Baikal, the "Blue Eye of Siberia." Lake Baikal is the deepest lake in the world and the largest freshwater lake in the world by volume.

The major aspects of the fresh water issue are scarcity and water pollution. An estimated 884 million people do not have access to safe water, and 2.5 million people have inadequate sanitation and waste disposal; at any given time, half of hospitalized patients are affected by waterborne illnesses. In 2006, the UN released a report suggesting that water scarcity is management-based rather than natural. This means that mankind is causing the shortage and the problems with safe water availability.

Technology can fix some of the problem. Most of these solutions are costly in money and energy, however. Israel spends about 53 cents per cubic meter to desalinize water, and Singapore spends a bit less, about 49 cents. Other countries that currently use or will be using desalinization to supply all or some of their water needs include Pakistan, China, India, Australia, Bermuda, the United States, and the United Arab Emirates.

Many non-profit and non-governmental organizations are lobbying governments to ensure safe water for all life on earth. Around the world, about two billion more people have access to safe drinking water than before 1990.

Above: Africa is one of the most vulnerable continents in terms of water shortage.

Human rights	6/10
Violence	5/10
World reach	8/10
Inevitability	7/10
Destruction	6/10
Average score	6.4/10

Patrick Bonneville: Currently, North Korea is the most isolated country in the world. Its leader, Kim Jong-il, and his family threaten the whole world with their nuclear program. Behind their puffed-up stance before the world and behind their well-armed and closely watched borders, there is a population living with minimal resources. In North Korea, nobody gets in, and nobody gets out, including those bringing humanitarian aid.

Above: Statue at the entrance to Pyongyang.

In 1995, the population of North Korea began to starve to death. The country went for four years in one of the worst food crises of our modern world, known as the North Korean famine. Close to three million North Koreans died. The rest of the world only became aware of the tragedy in 1999, at which time the international community succeeded in sending international aid to resolve the crisis. But for many families, it was too late. The North Korean leaders had failed to ask for help to protect and save their people.

After the Korean War, North Korea was very successful in building its self-sufficiency. Through considerable agricultural industrialization, and through "friendship prices" trade policies with the Soviet Union, the country had fed and maintained its people. In the 1990s, a series of natural disasters and the collapse of the Soviet Union led to the unthinkable: mass starvation.

As early as 1992, the North Korean government created propaganda programs in response to the crop failures: "Two meals per day are healthier than three." Rationing coupons soon were futile, as there was simply no food left to ration. In 1995, a series of devastating floods wiped out 40 percent of North Korea's arable land, severely affecting grain production. Tidal waves, followed by drought, plagued the country through 1996 and 1997. Despite his own opulent lifestyle, including special delicacies flown in fresh from abroad, Kim Jong-il's people were in distress. His country could no longer feed its people.

Even in the years since the crisis, North Korea has blocked most humanitarian aid from Western countries. As recently as June 2009, the United Nations World Food Program was only able to deliver food aid to about one-fifth of the population in need. The North Korean population continues to suffer from the isolation that Kim Jong-il has imposed.

Human rights	8/10
Violence	8/10
World reach	4/10
Inevitability	8/10
Destruction	4/10
Average score	6.4/10

The Falkland Islands War was initiated by Argentina against the British-controlled Falkland Islands, or the Islas Malvinas to Argentinians. Argentina launched an invasion of the islands on April 2, 1982.

The islands had been under British control and administration since 1833, however Argentina still claimed sovereignty over the land. Under Lieutenant General Leopoldo Galtieri, Argentina began a war that would end in a combined death toll of over 1,000 people and great military losses for Argentina.

Argentina's goals were transparently political. Galtieri's military junta was heavily criticized for financial misconduct and human rights abuses. The junta believed an Argentinian population united in a cause would lead to a united support for Galtieri. A plan was hatched to recuperate the islands as a rallying focus for the people. When a dispute broke out on the British-controlled island of South Georgia on March 19, 1982, Galtieri saw his chance and mobilized his naval forces to invade the capital of Port Stanley on April 2.

Galtieri had managed to position 10,000 troops on the various Falkland Islands by the end of April. The United Kingdom, under Prime Minister Margaret Thatcher, declared a war zone of 320 kilometers (200 miles) surrounding the islands and quickly assembled naval troops for retaliation. The UK had the support of most of Europe and, eventually, the United States and NATO.

Above: War veteran paying homage to fallen soldiers.

The war was intense. The Argentinian fleets were aggressive in the attempts to control the waters – both above and below – and had an admirable air presence. The UK had superior submarines and communication systems. On June 11, the UK launched a land attack to regain Port Stanley. The battles continued for three days. Argentina could not stave off the attacks and on June 14, 1982, Argentina surrendered. During several battles, the British had captured about 11,400 Argentine prisoners, all later released.

The defeat was the final blow to Galtieri's military government, and in 1983, the country returned to civilian rule. In 1990, Argentina and the United Kingdom restored full diplomatic relations. As for the Falkland Islands, the UK retains rule, while Argentina maintains its claim.

Human rights	8/10
Violence	6/10
World reach	6/10
Inevitability	9/10
Destruction	3/10
Average score	6.4/10

Patrick Bonneville: In 1956, the people of Hungary showed the world that they were not afraid of anyone. Hungarian history is there to prove it. In 1956, they had enough of the Soviet regime. They stood up against the empire. Nobody came to their defence. They paid a very high price for this uprising but they kept their dignity intact. I have a lot of respect for this country. Its has a unique heritage, a heritage of pride and honor.

The first breath of the Hungarian revolution was felt when Mátyás Rákosi was ousted as Communist Party leader in July 1956, following the death of Stalin in the Soviet Union. Under t rule since World War II, Hungary was one of the most repressed societies in the Eastern Block—some 350,000 officials and intellectuals had been flushed out of the country during Soviet-influenced rule.

A few months later, as part of a spontaneous nationwide uprising against Rákosi's replacement, Imre Nagy, and against Soviet-style communism, mass demonstrations took place in Budapest in October and early November. Demonstrators destroyed Soviet symbols and attacked the Party newspaper headquarters and demanded independence. President Nagy's request to the United Nations for help in leading Hungary to neutrality was ignored, and the Soviet Union quickly claimed control of Hungary, occupied Budapest, charged Nagy with treason, and effectively closed off the country to the outside world.

By the end of the quick Soviet siege, called "Operation Whirlwind," some 200,000 Hungarians had managed to escape to the West. Meanwhile, the Hungarian Communist Party reorganized and became the Hungarian Socialist Workers' Party under the leadership of János Kádár. Kádár lost no time in executing the participants of the revolution. Within a period of five years, about 2,000 people were killed and another 25,000 imprisoned.

"When Hungarians rose against their Soviet oppressors, the United States abandoned them."
—Author and professor Charles Gati, who escaped Hungary as a refugee

Above: The anniversary of the Hungarian revolution against communism is celebrated on October 23..

Human rights	9/10
Violence	9/10
World reach	3/10
Inevitability	7.5/10
Destruction	3/10
Average score	6.3/10

Patrick Bonneville: The entire world has criticized the American military prison at Guantanamo. Yes, the inmates were purportedly threats to America's and the world's security. Yes, they might have important information. But they also have the right to justice through a fair trial. The war against terrorism should be based on the foundation of human rights and international law. With Guantanamo, the USA lost the opportunity to show the world that the United States is fighting back, true to the principles of respect for human rights and international justice.

In 1903, Cuban President Tomás Estrada Palma and American President Theodore Roosevelt signed the Cuban-American Treaty, according the United States a perpetual lease on the land and surrounding water of the Guantánamo Bay area. The USA would have mining and naval station rights. In return, the Republic of Cuba would have ultimate sovereignty over the area and would have free passage through the water. The agreement included no intention for a prison.

Today, the Cuban government opposes the American naval base, claiming that it is not valid under international law. The so-called "cactus curtain" divides Guantánamo Bay from Cuba proper. Cuban troops planted the line of cactus in 1961. Both Cuban and American troops also placed an estimated 55,000 land mines in the no man's land around this border. During his presidency, President Bill Clinton ordered American land mines to be removed and replaced with sound sensors. The Cuban government, however, has not removed the minefield on its side of the border.

After the September 11, 2001 attacks on New York City by Al-Qaeda, the American Joint Task Force Guantànamo imprisoned Al-Qaeda or Taliban terrorist suspects at the naval base. This permitted the USA to deny these individuals any rights they would be entitled to as detainees under American legal jurisdiction. Some 775 detainees have been brought to the detention center since October 2001. Most prisoners have been released without charges; however, some 215 detainees are languishing at Guantanamo without charges laid against them.

Amnesty International, the United Nations and the European Union have all requested the closure of Guantánamo Bay.

Human rights	8/10
Violence	5/10
World reach	8/10
Inevitability	8/10
Destruction	2/10
Average score	6.2/10

Left: PKK border patrol.

The end of the 1970s saw the rise of ethnic separatist Kurdish rebels in Turkey. The conflict, which began in 1978 and continues to this day, is between the Republic of Turkey and the Kurdistan Worker's Party (PKK), an internationally recognized terrorist organization. The PKK are fighting for an independent state for Kurds currently living in Iraq.

Today, Turkey is home to about 14 million Kurds, close to 20 percent of the total Turkish population. Throughout the twentieth century, the government of Turkey has systematically segregated and isolated Kurds or banished them from the country. Several Kurdish uprisings in the 1920s, '30s and '40s did not result in Kurd integration and acceptance.

Nevertheless, the acts of the PKK are not seemingly in the best interests of the Kurd population, since the PKK is a terrorist group that uses violence as a means to secession. According to official Turkish statistics, between 1984 and 2008, 17,000 PKK members have been killed in armed insurgencies. The

Turkish army has lost 6,482 soldiers, and civilian casualties total 5,560. The conflict, which has spilled over into neighboring Iraq, has led to accusations of human rights abuses.

By 1978, the Kurdistan Workers Party began active urban war, operating out of Syria until 1984. Many of the violent attacks occurred in rural regions until 1993, when the organization moved into cities. Human rights organizations have documented crimes committed by the PKK, including the assassination of anyone believed to be in support of Turkey, including government workers, cultural and educational workers, as well as their families. Not to be outdone, the Turkish government is accused of ambushing Kurdish settlements, which has resulted in civilian deaths and the mass migration of families.

Today, Turkey is not a member of the European Union; these various human rights issues are part of the reason.

Human rights	8/10
Violence	8/10
World reach	3/10
Inevitability	7/10
Destruction	5/10
Average score	6.3/10

Kimberly Murray: In the end, history will show that Khomeini was a liar, a murderer, and a thief of humanity.

Tensions in pre-revolution Iran were at the boiling point when one of the world's worst terrorist attacks was committed. On August 20, 1978, in Abadan, Iran, the Cinema Rex theatre was deliberately set on fire. An estimated 422 people lost their lives in the blaze. The Iranian government blamed Islamic militants, others blamed Savak, the country's intelligence service. The day following the fire, some 10,000 mourners gathered for a mass funeral. The event was a trigger for the Iranian revolution.

Mohammad Reza Shah and his secret police, the Savak, had led Iran into Westernization and prosperity with the sale of oil. He and his government also dealt brutally with any opponents. On September 8, 1978, during a demonstration in Tehran, Savak security forces killed dozens of protestors. There were protests in almost every major city throughout the country as Iranian Muslims gathered to mourn past killings. Each subsequent gathering resulted in more murders.

Ayatollah Ruholla Khomeini, living in exile, led the revolution against the Shah, who fled the country in January 1979. Khomeini returned to Iran to lead a national referendum on April 1. An overwhelmingly huge majority voted to become a religious Islamic republic, with a new Islamic constitution and with Ayatollah Khomeini as its supreme spiritual leader. Many historians believe that this revolution was the beginning of the re-emergence of Islam as a worldwide political force.

Later that year, Iraq invaded Iran under the impression that Iran was now too weak to defend itself. Iran was strong enough to resist for six years, when a truce was initiated by the United Nations. The war cost billions of dollars and resulted in hundreds of thousands of deaths. Some statistics put the death toll as high as 950,000. Still, Khomeini was proud of Iran's performance in this war. It is believed he accepted the truce only because of the economic benefits it offered. Under his leadership, Iranian students took control of the U.S. Embassy in Tehran and held 52 people hostage for 444 days in response to the U.S. allowing the exiled Shah into their country for cancer treatments. Anti-Americanism has remained a fundamental stance of the religious Islamic government.

Khomeini ruled his people according to fundamental interpretations of the Qur'an until his death in 1989. For the West, he was the very face of radical Islam.

Human rights	6/10
Violence	8/10
World reach	5/10
Inevitability	8/10
Destruction	4/10
Average score	6.2/10

Patrick Bonneville: Some notable political prisoners from recent history are: Nelson Mandela, Mahatma Gandhi, Soviet nuclear physicist Andrei Sakharov, Zulfikar Ali Bhutto, Benazir Bhutto, South Korean Kim Dae-jung, Cuban Jorge Luis García Pérez. They were leaders who fought for the rights of their people. They changed humanity for the better, despite being locked in jail for years or decades. Their persistence and suffering made our world better. It is a shame today that similar humanitarian fighters are still being held in prison and silenced.

A political prisoner is someone held in prison or otherwise detained for his or her involvement in political activity. In a broadening of the term, human rights group Amnesty International began to refer to "prisoners of conscience" in the early 1960s. This term takes into account people who are held captive because of their race, religion, color, language, sexual orientation, belief, or lifestyle, so long as they have not used or advocated violence. Cuba's Dr. Oscar Elías Biscet González is serving a twenty-five-year prison sentence for his role in creating the Lawton Foundation, which advocates for the human rights and democratic freedoms of Cubans. He is in prison for allegedly committing crimes against the Republic of Cuba.

Uzbekistan's Sanjar Umarov is the chairman of the main opposition party to the current ruling government in Uzbekistan. He was arrested in 2006 for embezzlement; his supporters claim he was framed. He is currently in prison where his lawyer claims he is repeatedly drugged.

Myanmar's Aung San Suu Kyi is under house arrest by the current Burmese government. This legally elected Prime Minister was detained by the military and prevented from assuming her role. She has been under house arrest for fourteen of the last twenty years.

Probably once the youngest political prisoners in the world, China's Gedhun Choekyi Nyima, born in 1989, was named Tibet's eleventh Panchem Lama by the Dalai Lama, Tenzin Gyatso. Gedhun Choekyi Nyima and his family were removed from Tibet by the Chinese government after he was named Panchem Lama in 1995. His whereabouts are unknown.

Amnesty International continues to campaign for the release of these prisoners through its Prisoners of Conscience Appeal Fund.

"I am Juan Carlos Gonzalez Leiva, 39 years old, a blind Cuban lawyer and president of the Cuban Foundation of Human Rights, imprisoned since March 2, 2002 without a trial."
—Juan Carlos Gonzales Leiva, Holguin, Cuba, March 2004

Right: Campaign poster to free Aung San Suu Kyi on the European Parliament buildings in Brussels.

LIBERTÉ POUR
AUNG SAN SUU KYI
KHAROV 1990
oparl.europa.eu

Human rights	10/10
Violence	7/10
World reach	7/10
Inevitability	7/10
Destruction	0/10
Average score	6.2/10

Patrick Bonneville: In 1986, the world got an important reminder that nuclear power is dangerous, not only in weapons but as a source of energy.

Chernobyl is a city in northern Ukraine, near the border with Belarus. In 1986, the city was evacuated following a nuclear accident at the Chernobyl Nuclear Power Plant. Forty-nine deaths were reported to have occurred immediately, and about a thousand people absorbed lethal doses of radiation. Chernobyl ranks as the most costly disaster in modern history, topping $200 billion.

Earlier, in 1982, a partial core meltdown in the plant's reactor number one occurred. Because of its Cold War antagonism with the United States, the Soviet Union had an interest in maintaining an image of nuclear-power efficiency, and the accident was hushed up. The reactor was repaired and put back into service. The international community only learned of the incident years later.

On April 26, 1986, reactor number four exploded. Since Soviet nuclear plants did not have containment vessels, as do most Western plants, and radioactive dust billowed into the surrounding area—four hundred times more than was released with World War II's Hiroshima bomb. The city of Pripyat, built to house factory workers, was showered with fallout. Radiation contamination spread across the Ukraine, Russia, and Belarus, where 60 percent of the radioactive fallout landed. Nuclear rain fell as far as Ireland. Over twenty years later, lingering radiation and injuries from initial exposure mean that an accurate death toll may never be known.

Prior to the explosion, there had been serious safety violations. In fact, scientists working at the plant had actually shut off the Emergency Core Cooling System, the Local Automatic Control System, and the Emergency Power Reduction System. Some claim this was due to employee ignorance, others that it was due to arrogance and overconfidence. The International Atomic Energy Agency initially reported that the accident was due to human error. After investigation, they proposed that design flaws and poor plant construction may have been at fault.

The accident occurred following a scheduled shutdown for tests to determine how long the turbines would spin and supply power if the plant lost its main electrical power. A series of events, both automatic and manually directed, led the reactor core to become unstable as the test proceeded. Two explosions occurred: an initial steam explosion was followed by a fuel vapor

Left: Warning sign at the entrance of the city.
Right: Chernobyl is now a ghost town.

explosion, causing a nuclear excursion. These were followed by a reactor fire. Radioactive material was ejected into the atmosphere and continued to pollute the environment for the nine days the fire burned. The firefighters, police officers, and soldiers who were called to the scene—about 1,000 of them—absorbed lethal quantities of radiation. The city of Pripyat was evacuated within two days.

The real consequences of the accident will likely never be known. At the time, Soviet authorities responsible for Chernobyl claimed that the media had grossly exaggerated the effects of the accident. In fact, the Soviet Union neglected to inform the world of the accident after it happened; meteorological reports in Sweden led scientists there to conclude that a major disaster had occurred in Ukraine. It was only three days after the explosions that the Soviet Union officially acknowledged the incident to the whole world.

It is known that there has been an increase in cancer rates, thyroid problems, reproductive problems, and birth defects in the years following the disaster. Wild animals living within four kilometers (nearly 2.5 miles) of the plant died or could no longer reproduce, and forests surrounding the area were destroyed.

In a sign of the great resilience of nature, the region has now become a haven of sorts for wildlife, since there

are no permanent human inhabitants to threaten them. Tourists can easily obtain permission for guided tours of Pripyat, where the short-lived radioactive isotopes have dropped to relatively safe levels for short exposure.

"No reports were released until the third day after the Chernobyl explosion. Then, Swedish authorities correlated a map of enhanced radiation levels in Europe with wind direction and announced to the world that a nuclear accident had occurred somewhere in the Soviet Union. Before Sweden's announcement, the Soviet authorities were conducting emergency firefighting and clean-up operations but had chosen not report to the accident..."
—*The United Nations*

Human rights	3/10
Violence	0/10
World reach	8.5/10
Inevitability	9.5/10
Destruction	10/10
Average score	6.2/10

Patrick Bonneville: The world seems to be getting smaller in this era of globalization. Many borders have changed. People from the world over are now welcome to walk on the Great Wall in China. Yet elsewhere, new walls have been built to keep away "undesirable" people. There is a wall to keep Mexicans out of North America. One to keep the Bangladeshi out of India. And Israel has built one to seal itself off from the Palestinians and the Arab world. These are truly "walls of shame."

Above: 250 million people cross the Mexico - United States border every year.
Right: Painting on the Israeli West Bank Barrier. Similar paintings are common in the West Bank.

United States - Mexico

On October 26, 2006, the one hundred and ninth Congress of the United States passed the Secure Fence Act of 2006. The vote authorized the funding and possible construction of a fence along 700 miles of the U.S./Mexican border in California, Arizona, New Mexico, and Texas. The double-reinforced fence would be a strategy to keep out unwanted illegal immigrants arriving from Latin America, through Mexico. The fence would also restrict the illegal border crossings of vehicles carrying illicit drugs.

A few months later, twenty-five Texas landowners, including a corporation and a school district, refused to allow border fence surveys as an act of protest. In 2008, Hidalgo County in Texas finally agreed to the construction that combines the border fence with a levee to control flooding along the Rio Grande.

Although the fence will divide three American Indian tribal lands, the University of Texas at Brownsville, and countless private properties, construction has begun.

Israeli West Bank Barrier

The state of Israel is currently building a barrier along the Israeli West Bank; it will reach a length of 436 miles (703 kilometers). The construction, of which more than half is completed, is composed of eight-meter-high fencing with vehicle barrier trenches and concrete walls.

While two other similar Israeli barriers have already been built—the Israeli Gaza Strip Barrier and the Israeli-built wall separating Gaza from Egypt—they have remained in relative media obscurity. The new fence, however, has stirred up much controversy. Built along the West Bank and along the Green Line, which was decided in the 1949 armistice, it is touted to be a

"This wall would do damage to those of us living on both sides of the wall. This is a wall of shame that we neither want nor welcome. Texas is connected to Mexico by 23 bridges. Through these bridges we maintain our centuries-old friendships and blood ties with Mexico, as well as the trade and tourism which benefits this state and the entire United States of America."
—U.S. Senator Eddie Lucio, Texas

necessary means of protection for Israeli civilians from Palestinian terrorism. Opponents say the fence is illegal and is an attempt to annex Palestinian land. They argue that it violates international law and restricts the movement of Palestinians who need to travel in and out of the region. In 2004, the International Court of Justice declared the barrier to be "contrary to international law."

Israeli soldiers patrol gates along the wall which includes, on the Israeli side, land seized from Palestinians. Private land owners in the path of the barrier retain title to their land; the Israeli government pays them rent for use of their land and for any crop loss that results from the construction of the wall. It is reported that 60,000 olive and other fruit tress have been removed and replanted in order to make way for the barrier. Local businesses have not been so lucky. To date, 174 shops and stalls have been destroyed, and communities have lost the income generated from these businesses.

Above: According to the Israeli authorities, the West Bank wall has reduced the frequency of attacks by suicide bombers on Israeli soil.

"The United Nations General Assembly today voted overwhelmingly to demand that Israel comply with an advisory opinion issued earlier this month by the World Court, which declared the construction of a separation barrier in and around the West Bank to be illegal."
—United Nations, July 20, 2004

The Moroccan Wall
Officially known as the Berm of Western Sahara, the Morrocan Wall is almost 2,700 kilometers (1,677 miles) long. It acts as a separation between Moroccan-controlled areas and Polisario controlled areas. Polisario is a non-self governing territory that was a former colony of Spain. The purpose of the barrier is to prevent guerrilla fighters from the Polisario Front from agitating in Moroccan territory.

Cyprus
In 1974, Turkey constructed a fence along the northern edge of the United Nations Buffer Zone to separate the Turkish Republic of Northern Cyprus from the rest of Cyprus, populated by people of mostly Greek ancestry. The wall is 180 kilometers (111 miles) long and was built in violation of UN Security Council regulations. It is built mainly of barbed-wire fence, concrete wall segments, watchtowers, anti-tank ditches, and minefields. The buffer zone itself contains several villages and about 10,000 inhabitants. It is patrolled by UN peacekeeping forces.

Northern Ireland

Religion is the cause for the Peace Lines in cities across Northern Ireland. A series of variously-sized fences separate Catholic and Protestant neighbourhoods in Belfast, Derry, and other towns. Officials claim the fences help reduce sectarian violence. Some fences have gates and are manned by police and are closed at night.

Intended as a temporary measure to be removed in about six months, the first fences were built during the "Troubles" of the early 1970s. Today, however, there are still about forty barriers across the region. Even though the fences appear to represent segregation and intolerance, their presence is, for the most part, supported by residents.

Iran - Pakistan

This separation barrier is being built by Iran along its border with Pakistan to stop illegal border crossings, limit the flow of illegal drugs across the border, and serve as an anti-terrorist measure. Built to replace an older intermittent fence, the new barrier will span 700 kilometers (434 miles) and will be ten feet high and three feet wide. It is designed to include garrisons for troops and will have watchtowers. Although Iran and Pakistan do not currently have border disputes, critics are concerned that the fence will brew intolerance.

India

Since India is the destination for many illegal immigrates from poorer neighboring nations, it has developed a strategy of wall building to physically block the way. These border fences also serve to control the smuggling of goods, terrorists, and weapons.

The Bangledesh border fence will eventually stretch some 4,000 kilometers (2,485 miles) and will be constructed of concrete and barbed-wire fencing. The Indo-Burma barrier is intended to protect the 1,624 kilometer- (1,009 mile-) long border between India and Burma. The Indian Kashmir barrier was also conceived as an effort to curtail arms smuggling and infiltration by Pakistani-based separatist militants.

Ceuta border fence

This fence was constructed by the Spanish government in Ceuta, an autonomous city in Northern Africa that was colonized by Spain. It was built to restrict illegal immigration and smuggling. It is highly guarded, with underground cables connecting spotlights, noise and movement sensors, and video cameras. Police patrol the wall. Morocco has objected to the construction of the barrier.

Other similar barriers occur on the Kuwait-Iraq border and on the border between Yemen and Saudi Arabia.

Human rights	9/10
Violence	4/10
World reach	5/10
Inevitability	9.5/10
Destruction	3/10
Average score	6.1/10

Long controlled by Portugal, Angola gained its independence in 1975 and slipped immediately into civil war. Two main factions, the communist Popular Movement for the Liberation of Angola (MPLA) and the anti-communist National Union for Total Independence from Angola (UNITA) fought for control. A third movement, known as the FLEC, battled for independence of Cabinda, a province of Angola geographically separated by the DRC.

When Portugal pulled out of the country, the MPLA controlled the government, although UNITA was far more popular. The MPLA was supported by the Soviet Union and Cuba, while UNITA gained support with the United States, Brazil, and South Africa. The USSR and Cuba were eager to bring communism to Africa, and the sympathetic Angolan government was a perfect entry point. In November 1975, Cuba claimed victory in a battle at Ebo against South Africa. This defeat increased South Africa's desire to intensify its involvement in the country, since it was eager to maintain control of its joint neighbor, Namibia.

With the increased South African interest, Cuba began withdrawing in 1989. The American and South African-backed UNITA gained ground and began to develop governmental policies. By 1992, the country was ready for an election, and the MPLA won. The win led only to more violence as civil war once again enveloped the country. An estimated two million people were forced to flee in the two years that followed.

Above: The flag of Angola.

The United Nations mediated another peace agreement, which did not hold for long. While the civil war began as a conflict of ideology, by the mid-1990s it had evolved into a battle for the control of the country's resources, specifically the MPLA-controlled oil industry and the UNITA-controlled diamond industry.

By 2002, UNITA was officially declared a political party and demobilized its armed forces. Negotiations began to bring all members of the conflict to the table to form the Government of National Unity and Reconstruction (GURN). By 2002, over 500,000 people had lost their lives, and the country was left peppered with land mines. The planting of more than 20 million land mines destroyed the agricultural livelihoods of many. The country slipped into extreme poverty. Today, the country is still living with the effects of this brutal civil war.

Human rights	9/10
Violence	9/10
World reach	1/10
Inevitability	5/10
Destruction	6.5/10
Average score	6.1/10

Left: The European Union requires member states not to practice the death penalty.

The death penalty is the judicial process of killing a person for retribution, general deterrence from crime, or incapacitation (taking away a person's ability to commit further harm). It is also known as capital punishment or execution. Although it has been practiced throughout history and continues to be a means of justice in many states, capital punishment garners criticism and creates controversy around the world today.

The four most populous countries carry out the death penalty: the People's Republic of China, India, the United States, and Indonesia. In 2008 the worldwide execution rate was at least 2,390 per year. At the end of 2007, there were 25,000 prisoners waiting on death row, most of them in Pakistan and the USA. Amnesty International confirmed 470 executions in 2007 in China, although some evidence points to a much higher number, perhaps as many as 6,000.

The United Nations Convention on the Rights of the Child prohibits the death penalty for juveniles. The relevant article of the convention has been signed and ratified by all countries except Somalia and the United States. In Somalia, a 13-year girl was buried to her neck in the ground and then stoned to death in front of a crowd of at least 1,000. She had allegedly pleaded guilty to adultery and had "requested" her punishment. Amnesty International learned, however, that she had been arrested after she reported being raped by three men.

Even though Iran ratified the convention, that country is the world's biggest executioner of young offenders, who account for two-thirds of all juvenile executions. Iran has about 140 people on death row in total. Juveniles in Saudi Arabia and Yemen have also been executed in flagrant contradiction to international laws.

Overall, the public's opinion about the death penalty practice is split: an international Gallup poll conducted in 2000 found that 52 percent of respondents favored the death penalty. Apparently, terrorism also led to an overwhelming demand for the execution of the guilty. In China, Japan, and Singapore, cultural beliefs mean that people favor executions as a way to restore the natural order.

Human rights	9/10
Violence	8/10
World reach	6.5/10
Inevitability	7/10
Destruction	0/10
Average score	6.1/10

Patrick Bonneville: The place where this Union Carbide factory stood should be torn apart and the soil cleaned up. Then a great memorial should be built to remind the world that this cannot be allowed to happen again. All of this should be paid for by the Dow Chemical Company, the parent corporation. Investors who include Dow in their portfolios should seriously consider what their shares say about their values.

On December 3, 1984, the Union Carbide pesticide plant in the town of Bhopal, India, spewed 42 tonnes (46 tons) of toxic methyl insocyanate (MIC) gas into the atmosphere, exposing more than 500,000 people to toxic gases. Officially, within the first 72 hours, 2,259 people were killed. Unofficially, the death toll figure should be adjusted upward, to between 8,000 and 10,000. In 1993, nine years after the incident, the International Medical Commission was founded in order to examine and respond to the long-term health effects of the disaster.

Above: Bhopal victims have been demanding justice for years.

The Union Carbide India, Limited (UCIL) factory had been in operation since 1969 and produced the pesticide carbayl, trademarked as Sevin. The factory added a second product, methyl insocyanate (MIC) in 1979, even though studies have shown that the Union Carbide Corporation did not know how to properly handle the gas. The accident may have happened when large amounts of water entered a tank containing a large amount of MIC. The temperature in the tank soared to over 200 degrees Celsius (392 °F), and toxic fumes spread through the city.

The fumes included a mixture of gases. The dense chemical cocktail was a cloud that spread throughout the city, low to the ground. Children and shorter people were vulnerable to higher concentrations of the gas, and those who did not own a car to escape the city were exposed for a longer period.

The thousands of sudden deaths were a shock. There were mass funerals, mass cremations, and thousand of bodies were thrown into the Narmada river. About 170,000 people were treated at hospitals, and 2,000 goats, buffalo, and other animals had to be collected and buried. Leaves turned yellow and dropped from trees, and food supplies became scarce.

An estimated 20,000 deaths have been attributed to the accident in the years since the disaster. Up to 200,000 people have permanent injuries; most of them related to the eyes, lungs, and heart. There are also cases of immune-system weaknesses, reproductive difficulties, and birth defects. The American- and UK-funded clinic Sambhavna treats victims of the disaster.

The Union Carbide Company responded by sending aid and international medical experts to assist in the aftermath of the accident. They also donated $2 million to the Indian Prime Minister's disaster relief fund. The company also established the Employees' Bhopal Relief Fund two months after the disaster; it raised over $5 million for relief efforts. Three years after the event, they contributed another $4.6 million in interim humanitarian relief. They eventually sold their shares in UCIL and created a charitable trust in order to build a local hospital. The hospital opened in 2001 and caters to eye, heart, and lung problems.

Warren Anderson, Chairman and CEO of Union Carbide, was arrested in India on charges of manslaughter for the role of his company in the accident. He had traveled to India under promise from its government that he would not be arrested. He was released on bail on December 7,1984, and left the country to avoid a trial and a ten-year prison sentence. He has since refused to return. It is likely that India has not pressed the USA for his extradition so as not to cause trade and investment to suffer.

Investigations into the disaster led to many theories as to how the accident occurred. It was postulated that water got into the tanks while workers were cleaning them; because of poor maintenance, water could have seeped in through leaky valves. Plant management, however, proved this was not possible through a demonstration to the Central Bureau of Investigation. UCC put forth the theory that the incident was an act of sabotage by a disgruntled employee, even as the company accepted "moral responsibility" for the incident. The investigation team could not find evidence to back the company's claim of sabotage. What was clear was that no evacuation plan had been developed in case of an emergency; safety systems had been cut back due to poor sales; and that MIC is one of the most toxic substances known to humans.

The Indian government closed the plant to outsiders, including to representatives from UCC, which had a 51 percent share in the company. The government also refused to release information to the public. The Indian Council of Scientific and Industrial Research report was released a shocking fifteen years after the disaster, and studies on the accident's health effects were sealed until after 1994. The official position taken was that the incident did not cause any long-term health effects.

Human rights	6/10
Violence	2/10
World reach	5/10
Inevitability	10/10
Destruction	7/10
Average score	6.0/10

Human rights	10/10
Violence	6/10
World reach	5/10
Inevitability	8/10
Destruction	1/10
Average score	6.0/10

Patrick Bonneville: Homosexuals must be very careful in many countries of the world, where they are persecuted. Laws against homosexuality can be surprisingly harsh.

Although homosexuality has existed since the beginning of humanity, there are very few societies that tolerate it. In Ancient Greece, for example, homosexuality among male citizens did not replace the heterosexual union. Rather, it was seen as a form of "coming of age" in which older men would initiate younger men into adulthood. There were no equivalent practices for women. In ancient Jewish scripture—in Leviticus, which dates back to at least 550 BC—sexual relations between men were illegal and punishable by death. Some pagan cultures practiced same-sex intercourse as a part of religious ceremony and not as a lifestyle choice. In modern history, the creation of laws that restrict homosexual practices were nearly standard. In most cases, they were justified by religious scriptural references.

Today, homosexuality is subject to imprisonment in most African countries, with the exception of Rwanda, Madagascar, South Africa, Equatorial Guinea, and Chad. In Sudan, Mauritania, and Nigeria, the death penalty is leveled against people caught in homosexual activities. Gay tourists need to be careful when travelling throughout the Caribbean as well: Belize, Antigua, Barbados, and Jamaica do not welcome gays. Cuba does. In the Middle East, gays in Saudi Arabia, United Arab Emirates, Yemen, and Iran can be served the death penalty. Islamic states argue that anti-homosexuality laws are in place to protect the teachings of their religion and to protect the morality and virtue of their people. In some countries where homosexuality between men is illegal, lesbianism is permitted. This is the case in Fiji, Singapore, Uzbekistan, Grenada, the Seychelles, and Kenya.

International human rights organizations lobby for the end of laws condemning homosexuality. Human Rights Watch and Amnesty International, along with the United Nations Human Rights Committee, hold the opinion that choice about sexual orientation is an inherent right and laws prohibiting homosexuality are a violation against the Universal Declaration of Human Rights.

Several countries have recently legalized same-sex marriages: the Netherlands (2001), Belgium (2003), Spain (2005), Canada (2005), South Africa (2006), Norway (2009), and Sweden (2009). Since the U.S. invasion of Iraq, the Iraqi government has made homosexuality legal.

"In Iran we don't have homosexuals like in your country. In Iran we do not have this phenomenon. I don't know who's told you that we have this."
—Iranian President Mahmoud Ahmadinejad, in his famous speech at Columbia University in New York City, September 2007

Left: Rainbow flag, symbol of the Pride movement.

Human rights	8/10
Violence	7.5/10
World reach	4/10
Inevitability	8/10
Destruction	2/10
Average score	5.9/10

Patrick Bonneville: Students have often been at the center of the fight for a just world. In 1989, Chinese students stood up for their fellow students, their people, and their nation. They were crushed by the military, but the events of June 1989 showed the world that China was changing—that Chinese people will fight for their rights.

China showed its ugly side to the world in 1989. On April 14, students peacefully gathered to mourn the death of Hu Yaobang, a pro-democracy leader near Tiananmen Square in Beijing. The students and the intellectuals who joined them had appreciated Hu Yaobang's pro-market, anti-corruption politics. Forced to retire from the Chinese government in 1987 because of his convictions, he had just died of a heart attack at age seventy-three. The public demanded a state funeral, but the government's slow response led people to create their own public memorials.

In the weeks following Yaobang's death, an estimated one million people gathered at Tiananmen Square to call for economic change and to decry the authoritarian government. There were hunger strikes and calls for freedom of the press, and protests across China. The government accepted only to speak to a very select group of students, those sympathetic to its policies.

On June 4, the Chinese government issued an order to have Tiananmen Square cleared of protestors. Military tanks moved in. The Red Cross reported that 2,500 were killed and up to 10,000 injured. Following the slaughter of students, the authorities then began to make arrests. Members of the foreign press were either deported or strictly controlled. Government officials who showed sympathy for the events were purged. The international community condemned the actions and announced sanctions against China.

Four Chinese student arrests made headlines. Wang Dan, Chai Ling, Zhao Changqing, and Wuer Kaixi were student leaders who demanded democratic change. Dan was arrested and sent to prison. He eventually won the right to emigrate to the USA. Changqing was also sent to prison but was released after six months. His continued demonstrations led to another arrest and imprisonment. Kaixi escaped to Taiwan, and Ling managed to escape to Paris and eventually to the USA, where she lives today and remains an active voice for democracy in China.

Perhaps one of the most iconic images of this event is what the media referred to as "Tank Man." This unknown hero defied the Chinese government and its military by placing himself directly in the path of one of the tanks deployed to disperse the protesters. On June 5, as the tanks approached Tiananmen Square, Tank Man stood defiantly and moved each time the tank would try to pass. The police eventually removed him by force. The international community demanded that the Chinese government prove he remained alive, but he was never seen again.

Left: Performance art in Hong Kong at the 20th anniversary of the Tiananmen Square Massacre.

"I believe in equal rights for everyone according to their circum-
tances . . . Women do have rights, but they are based on our view
of their obligations in life."
—Dr. Saleh al-Sheikh, Minister for Islamic affairs in Saudi Arabia

Human rights	9/10
Violence	6/10
World reach	3/10
Inevitability	10/10
Destruction	1/10
Average score	5.8/10

Human rights, specifically women's rights, in Saudi Arabia have been questioned by Western countries and human rights organizations the world over. The Saudi government aims to restrict the interaction of women in public and in male circles. Their belief is that women should be in the home, caring for husband and family. If she does choose to work, she must have permission from her husband and she must continue all expected duties in the household. Houses and buildings have separate entrances for men and women, and if women are to be in public places where men may be, they must be escorted by a male relative. The religious police (the Mutawa) actively enforce the laws, which Western companies operating in the country are forced to abide by.

Discrimination against women extends to legal representation. Under Saudi law, a woman may not defend herself in court unless the alleged criminal act did not occur with any men around. A woman's testimony is not considered. According to current Saudi law, God created men superior, therefore women must testify only that which a man tells them.

It is very difficult for a Saudi woman to legally protect herself. Cases of assault, rape, or other such crimes tend to be swept under the rug. A recent case led to 200 lashings of a female gang rape victim, who was judged to be guilty for being in a car that did not belong to a male relative.

Left: The *mutawwa*, religious police in Saudi Arabia, can arrest women who do not wear the hijab.

In Saudi Arabia, no woman can move freely without the express permission of her husband or male guardian, if she is unmarried. Nor is she allowed to drive. A woman may receive medical attention only when permitted by her husband or male guardian, and she may only be seen by a female doctor. Saudi women are encouraged to wear the niqab, a black garment that covers the body, revealing only the eyes. Higher education is segregated in Saudi Arabia, although the government does support education for both sexes. Women make up an estimated 70 percent of university enrolment, but they make up a mere 7 percent of the workforce.

Prior to 2006, women were not granted the right to hold an identity card; their names were added to their fathers' cards. In 2006 the government issued an ordinance that required all women to have their own photo-ID cards. And while this may seem to be an advance, it is apparently yet another way for the Saudi government to force women into isolation: under Saudi religious law, it is forbidden for women to have their picture taken—this makes it virtually impossible for women to have their own identity cards.

Although Saudi Arabia signed the UN Convention on the Elimination of all Forms of Discrimination against Women (CEDAW) in 2001, there is reason to believe that what the government says it is doing and what it is actually doing are very different.

25000000

AC3064582

10 000 000 RESERVE BANK OF

TEN MILLION
DOLLARS

on or before

100 000 RESERVE BANK OF ZIMBABWE 100 0

Pay the bearer on demand

ONE HUNDRED
THOUSAND DOLLARS

on or before
31st July 2007

for the Reserve Bank of
Zimbabwe

Issue date: 1st August 2006

BEARER CHEQUE

02022909

Dr. G Gono
Governor

100 000

AV90722

SPECIAL AGRO-CHEQUE

HUNDRED

ON DOLLARS

st December 2008
Bank of Zimbabwe
st July 2008

100

BILLION

10 000 000

02022900

100000000000 RESERV

AA1027601

Human rights	5/10
Violence	5/10
World reach	5/10
Inevitability	10/10
Destruction	4/10
Average score	5.8/10

Patrick Bonneville: If you were born in Zimbabwe, one of the most beautiful lands of the world, your life expectancy is half of that in many other countries.

Zimbabwe is a country in the southern part of Africa that has been the center of civil uprisings for generations. Known as Rhodesia under British colonial rule, it asserted independence from the United Kingdom in 1965. Its sovereignty was challenged by its colonizer and was officially recognized only in 1980. Its roughly 13 million citizens speak any of three official languages: English, Shona, and Ndebele.

President Robert Mugabe has been accused of economic mismanagement and grave human rights abuses. His tyrannical government suppresses the free press and he has been known to brutalize opposition. As a result, popularity for Prime Minister Morgan Tsvangirai and his Movement for Democratic Change is on the rise.

President Mugabe's redistribution of land owned by non-native Africans to members of the black Zimbabwean elite began in 2000. The compulsory land redistribution entailed the intimidation and brutalization of "white" farmers. It is believed that thousands were murdered; however, Mugabe refutes this claim. In 2002, The Commonwealth of Nations suspended Zimbabwe's participation because of such charges of human rights abuse.

Left: The country's inflation rate reached 90 sextillion percent in 2008.

As a result of the land redistribution, the country has seen a sharp decline in agricultural exports. Zimbabwe had long relied on these exports for its economy, and without them, the country has fallen into a shortage of hard currency. Hyperinflation and shortages of fuel and consumer goods has meant growth in slum developments and homelessness. Health statistics also reflect the decline of Zimbabwe into disorder and death: today, the life expectancy for males is thirty-seven years. In 1990, it was sixty. Women have an average life span of thirty-four years. Infant mortality is 81 per 1,000 live births, compared to 4.8 for Canada or 2.9 for Hong Kong. Equally devastating are HIV statistics; an estimated 1.8 million Zimbabweans have HIV/AIDS.

"The only white man you can trust is a dead white man."
—President Robert Mugabe

"Over the last decade, Zimbabwe's ruling party, the Zimbabwe African National Union-Patriotic Front (ZANU-PF), has progressively and systematically compromised the independence and impartiality of Zimbabwe's judiciary and public prosecutors, and instilled one-sided partisanship into the police. Since 2000 it has purged the judiciary, packed the courts with ZANU-PF supporters and handed out 'gifts' of land and goods to ensure the judges' loyalty."
—Human Rights Watch, 2008

Patrick Bonneville: This could have been the land of the free, a tropical paradise where slaves stood up to their owners and built their own nation. They were the first to fight and win. This nation was built by brave and courageous men and women. In January 2010, after one of the most damaging earthquakes in history hit the country, the whole world stepped forward to help Haitians and rebuild the country.Haiti is on the Wall of Shame because of its political instability, corruption, and violence, as well as for environmental destruction, economic woes, and poor education opportunities for its citizens.

Haiti is a presidential republic with a constitution modelled after those of the United States and France. In February 2004, a coup against elected president Jean-Bertrand Aristide led to his ousting, and he was forced into exile in South Africa. Aristide claims he was kidnapped by the U.S. and French governments, who allege that he was involved in drug trafficking.

The coup was an act of revenge on the part of the brother of gang leader Amiot Métayer, who died in 2003. Buteur Métayer took charge of the Cannibal Army, renaming it the National Revolutionary Front for the Liberation of Haiti, and promptly took control of the city of Gonaïves. After the secret departure of Aristide, the UN quickly sent in peacekeeping troops. An estimated 7,000 peacekeepers from the USA, France, Canada, Brazil, Chili, Argentina, Jordan, Morocco, Nepal, Peru, Philippines, Spain, Sri Lanka, and Uruguay flooded the small nation. Following Aristide's exile, a former colleague, Réné Préval won a general election and assumed the Presidency.

President Préval's current government is under harsh criticism for the severe food crisis that has plagued the nation over the past few years. Many independent organizations and humanitarian agencies consistently rank Haiti as one of the most corrupt countries on the planet. In 2006, the Corruptions

Above: In 2008, La Promesse College collapsed, killin 93 young students. The tragedy was not caused by an earthquake, but by poor construction.

Right: Satellite image of the border between Haiti and the Dominican Republic. Haiti is on the left, where there is no more vegetation to be seen.

Perceptions Index ranked Haiti as the worst in the world. The International Red Cross put Haiti as number 155 out of 159 countries examined.

Environmentally, Haiti has been virtually destroyed. In 1925, Haiti was a lush land with healthy forests covering an estimated 60 percent of the country. Widespread logging for the production of charcoal has reduced forest acreage to a mere 2 percent of Haitian land. Erosion caused by deforestation is severe and has caused the ruin of fertile farmland. Haiti is also prone to tropical storms, flooding, and mudslides. As recently as 2008, three hurricanes and one severe tropical storm battered the country within a span of two months. The storms killed 331 people and left about 800,000 in dire need of humanitarian aid. Because of the country's already weak infrastructure and food distribution, as well as its political corruption, thousands of people suffer needlessly after such natural disasters.

Today, Haiti is the poorest country in the Western Hemisphere. Since the January 2010 earthquake, it is hoped that the international community will help Haiti develop a sustainable economy and rebuild its towns. We hope the country will, one day soon, see an end to its misery.

"The border between Haiti and the Dominican Republic (D.R.) is more than just a political boundary. It also reflects the large amount of deforestation that has occurred on the Haitian side of the border. One can easily see from satellite imagery the lush forests still thriving on the D.R. side of the border, which is in sharp contrast to the Haitian side of the border."
—NASA

"Haiti is a fragile state where armed gangs can be used to stir up trouble for political reasons and abject poverty fuels discontent."
—Rob Drouen, head of the ICRC delegation in Haiti

Human rights	6/10
Violence	8/10
World reach	3/10
Inevitability	7/10
Destruction	5/10
Average score	5.8/10

"Scores and scores of bodies—hundreds of bodies—wearing red dresses, blue T-shirts, green blouses, pink slacks, children's polka-dotted jumpers. Couples with their arms around each other, children holding parents. Nothing moved."
—TIME magazine correspondent Donald Neff, witness to the aftermath of the Jonestown mass suicide

Human rights	8/10
Violence	9/10
World reach	1/10
Inevitability	9/10
Destruction	2/10
Average score	5.8/10

In 1955, the American James Warren Jones founded a religious organization known as the Peoples Temple. By the mid-1970s, there were branches in more than a dozen locations throughout California, and its headquarters had been moved from Indiana to San Francisco. One of Jones' projects was the Peoples Temple Agricultural Project in Guyana where, in November 1978, he persuaded 918 of his faithful followers to commit mass suicide. Other people were murdered there by followers of Jones, including journalists accompanying Congressman Leo Ryan, who had come to investigate human rights abuses by Jones. Until the September 11, 2001 terrorist attacks, it was the greatest civilian loss of life in a non-natural disaster in the United States.

The demagogue Jones created the Peoples Temple after becoming disillusioned with the limitations of other organizations, such as the Communist Party of the United States of America and the Methodist church. With his newly created Peoples Temple, he used faith healings to attract a congregation and generate an income that would allow him to advance his social ideas.

Jones became obsessed with the notion that the world was about to engage in a nuclear war. He preached that his followers must flee to a new location to be safe from the fallout. Initially, he chose northern California, where he and his church flourished. When San Francisco Chronicle reporter Marshall Kilduff wrote an article exposing physical, emotional, and sexual abuse in the Peoples Temple, Jones moved with as many members as possible to some leased land in the South American nation Guyana, where his group established their agricultural project. The settlement was called Jonestown, in his honor.

By late 1978, more than 900 people had settled in Jonestown. Jones had attracted them with the promise of a land where all members, especially blacks, would be free from the oppression of the outside world. When Congressman Leo Ryan and a support group landed in Guyana on November 17 to investigate alleged abuses, several Temple members requested to leave with Ryan. On November 18, Ryan accompanied the members to the local airport, from where they would leave together. While boarding the plane, they were attacked by Temple security. There were five deaths—three journalists, a temple member, and Congressman Ryan.

That evening, James Warren Jones convinced over 900 people (including more than 270 children) to drink cyanide-laced Flavor-Aid. With that act, Jones murdered 918 people. No cameras recorded the mass suicide pact, although Jones left a forty-four-minute cassette tape on which he was recorded urging followers to commit "revolutionary suicide."

"We are not committing suicide; it's a revolutionary act."
—Excerpt of Jones' final speech, just before the mass suicide

Part of the United Kingdom, Northern Ireland is located on the northern tip of the Island of Ireland, which it shares with the Republic of Ireland to the south. It has about 1,800,000 inhabitants, or about 30 percent of the island's population.

"The Troubles" is how the Irish refer to the series of violent political and religious conflicts in Northern Ireland—and, at times, in parts of England, the Republic of Ireland, and mainland Europe—that began in the late 1960s and ended with the Belfast Agreement of 1998. The civil war was between those nationalists wishing for "home rule" and who were predominantly Catholic, and those wishing to remain part of the UK, or the unionists, who were mostly Protestant. Despite the 1998 agreement, sporadic violence continues.

There is a much longer history of antagonism, however. It dates back to the seventeenth century and the arrival of

Scottish and British settlers, known as planters, who settled on land rightfully owned by native Irish families. Later, with the official merging of Ireland into the United Kingdom in 1801, the unionist-nationalist conflict began in earnest.

Although the Catholic Irish continued to live in the region as a minority, Protestant Britain dominated politically and socially, then as now. Beginning in the 1960s, when Protestant unionists armed themselves in an illegal paramilitary organization called the Ulster Volunteer Force, the Troubles erupted. The conflict between the UVF and the older Provisional Irish Republican Army (IRA) would go on to claim the lives of about 3,500 people.

On January 30, 1972, in Derry, members of the First Battalion of the British Parachute Regiment shot at twenty-seven civil rights protesters during a protest march. The event is referred to as "Bloody Sunday." Thirteen people died immediately, while another died later from injuries sustained in the gunfire. There were many witnesses, including journalists, who testified that none of the victims were carrying weapons. Most of the victims were teenagers, and five were shot in the back.

Above: Political propaganda in Belfast, Northern Ireland

Human rights	6/10
Violence	8/10
World reach	5/10
Inevitability	6/10
Destruction	4/10
Average score	5.8/10

Organizers of the protest march say there were 30,000 marchers, whereas the Widgery Tribunal estimated there were between 3,000 and 5,000. The march was initially planned to bring the activists to the Derry Guildhall but was rerouted to avoid army barricades. A small group of teenagers broke through the barricades and began to march on the Guildhall, where they threw stones and shouted at the British troops. The troops retaliated with tear gas, rubber bullets, and a water canon, purportedly to disperse the crowd. But in late afternoon, the army was given the order to fire live rounds. One man was killed as he ran away from the advancing troops. The violence escalated, and over a hundred rounds were fired directly into the fleeing crowds under the command of Major Ted Loden. A cease-fire was ordered but ignored. Twelve people took bullets, and armored vehicles ran down two others.

The immediate official response was that the British troops had reacted to suspected IRA threats of bombs. Other marchers, local residents, and British and Irish journalists alike maintain that the soldiers fired into an unarmed crowd. They also claim that the soldiers fired at people fleeing the scene and even at those tending the wounded. The soldiers were not fired upon—none were wounded and no bullets or nail bombs were ever found to support British claims.

Bloody Sunday was twice investigated by the British government. The 1972 Widgery Tribunal cleared soldiers and British authorities, and the Saville Inquiry will release its findings early in 2010. After Bloody Sunday, the IRA's membership increased dramatically and public support skyrocketed.

"In 1969 the London government deployed the British army in an attempt to restore order. Initially many in the Catholic population saw the army as their protectors from the Northern Ireland state and a repressive majority population. For more militant nationalists, however, the introduction of the army restored the traditional republican symbol of oppression—British troops on Irish soil."
—John Darby, founding director of INCORE (International Conflict research)

Right: Northern Ireland.

Kimberly Murray: There is probably no land upon this earth that has not suffered from natural disasters. From a humanitarian standpoint, what counts is the reaction from local, national, and international governments and organizations. As we will see with this event, it could have—and should have—been alleviated.

The Great Chinese Famine, known in China as the Three Years of Natural Disasters, occurred between 1958 and 1961. Official Chinese statistics declare the death toll from starvation to be 15 million; independent research puts this figure much higher, at about 36 million.

China maintains that the famine was a natural phenomenon, even if some small clerical errors compounded the situation. The international viewpoint, however, is that Chinese policy was largely responsible for the famine and consequent deaths. It is generally agreed that famine is not simply a result of reduced food production but also of poor food distribution.

Mao Zedong's national restructuring plan, known as the Great Leap Forward, included the transition of China from an agricultural society to a communist one. Farming became a government enterprise—private plots were forbidden and their owners were politically and socially punished. Farmers were forced to give up agriculture to work in other industries, including iron mining and steel fabrication.

The country might have been able to overcome such an error, but the poor crop yields and bad farm management were compounded by adverse weather patterns. The natural flooding of the Yellow River in 1959 resulted in extreme crop failure, killing an estimated two million people. Some consider this event one of the top deadliest natural disasters of the twentieth century. Drought also affected just over half the farmland, and grain production dropped by about 70 percent. The famine continued through 1961 and ended only once China stopped its Great Leap Forward and began the de-collectivization of agriculture.

Human rights	5/10
Violence	2/10
World reach	4/10
Inevitability	9/10
Destruction	9/10
Average score	5.8/10

"With so many people starving to death, you and I will be held responsible by history. Cannibalism is bound to end up in history books!"
—Liu Shaoqi, warning Mao Zedong

Patrick Bonneville: Saddam's folly ended up an ecological disaster, an aspect of the war that is rarely mentioned.

In the fall of 1990, the United States mounted a military response to Iraq's invasion of Kuwait, a tiny oil-rich country that Iraq had invaded in August of that year. The United States, Saudi Arabia, the United Kingdom, Egypt, and thirty other countries rallied to banish Saddam Hussein's Iraqi forces, with Saudi Arabia paying for the majority of the costs. The conflict also included United Nations Security Council economic sanctions against Iraq. Iraq had invaded Kuwait for its oil, some of which, they claimed, the Kuwaitis had been stealing from Iraqi wells.

"Unfortunately, we were dealing with someone who had no regard for human life, and no regard for the environment, in the person of Saddam Hussein. But now we have to deal wtih the consequences of his ecoterrorism."
—Nancy Pelosi, 1991

Above: USAF aircraft fly over Kuwaiti oil fires, set by the retreating Iraqi army during Operation Desert Storm in 1991.

On January 21, 1991, the Iraqi military caused an oil spill in the Persian Gulf that has been called the worst in history. The Iraqi forces opened valves at Sea Island, an oil-tanker wharf, in order to prevent the American military from landing on shore. Some say up to 462 million gallons of oil was spilled, causing a five-inch-thick oil slick that was 101 miles long and 42 miles wide. Despite debates about the actual volume of the spill, figures place it at five to twenty-seven times the size, in gallons spilled, of the Exxon Valdez oil spill. It caused considerable damage to wildlife in the Persian Gulf, especially in areas surrounding Kuwait and Iraq.

According to a study sponsored by UNESCO and several oil-producing countries, the spill did little long-term damage. About half the oil evaporated, a million barrels were recovered, and two to three million barrels' worth washed ashore, mainly in Saudi Arabia.

"As the 1990-1991 Gulf War showed, conflicts have devastating effects on the environment, biodiversity and the quality of life of local people long after the cessation of hostilities",
—Dr Michael Rands, BirdLife International, 2003

Human rights	1/10
Violence	4/10
World reach	6/10
Inevitability	8/10
Destruction	9.5/10
Average score	5.7/10

Mozambique lies on the Indian Ocean in Eastern Africa. South Africa and Swaziland border it to the south, Zimbabwe and Malawi to the west, and Tanzania to the north. For centuries, Mozambique was under Portuguese colonial rule, and in 1975 it was granted independence. A sixteen-year long civil war began, ending only in 1992. Some five million civilians were displaced and an estimated 900,000 were killed, including soldiers.

At the time of its independence, the Front for Mozambique Liberation, known as FRELIMO, a Marxist-Leninist government, began to rebuild the country. A second group known as the Mozambique Resistance Movement, or RENAMO, was gaining support from the white-minority governments of South Africa and Rhodesia. RENAMO was active in preventing trade with Zimbabwe.

FRELIMO politics, inversely, included hostility to the white-minority governments of Rhodesia and South Africa. The group found solidarity with Zimbabwean nationalist guerrillas in Rhodesia (ZANLA) and the African National Congress of South Africa (the ANC). The stage for internal conflict was set: FRELIMO, with support from ZANLA and the ANC, against RENAMO, with support from White South Africa and Rhodesia.

Following two years of full-scale guerrilla war and Zimbabwean control of Mozambique, RENAMO moved ahead with a movement that would lead FRELIMO President Samora Machel and South African President P.W. Botha to sign the Nkomati agreement, which effectively shut down any ANC support to the country. The period saw many deaths from fighting and starvation.

The intensity of the conflict dwindled toward the end of the 1980s. As a result of the death of Machal, under suspicious circumstances, FRELIMO began to move away from the Marxist leaning of the Soviet Union and increased pressure from South Africa. New American support for RENAMO led to the creation of a new constitution in July of 1989. One year later, in July of 1990, mediators from the Italian government and leaders from the Catholic Church met with FRELIMO and RENAMO to begin peace negotiations. A cease-fire was declared in December of that year, although tensions remained.

The world's political climate was changing: the cold war had ended, apartheid had been dismantled, and white supremacy in Africa was fading. The country was broke and broken; the war had used all its resources and forced thousands to flee. A UN peacekeeping force spent two years aiding the country in the transition to peace. Today, Mozambique is relatively democratic, with the FRELIMO party holding a majority government opposite the RENAMO minority.

Right: The suffering of the Mozambican Civil War and the Mozambique War of Independence have left important wounds on many generations.

Human rights	5/10
Violence	8/10
World reach	2/10
Inevitability	7/10
Destruction	6/10
Average score	5.7/10

"Without Jerusalem, the land of Israel is as a body without a soul."
—Elhanan Leib Lewinsky (1857-1910), Hebrew writer and Zionist leader

Patrick Bonneville: Jerusalem could have become the greatest city of the world, a symbol of love and faith for all human beings. Instead, it is a symbol of hatred, revenge, injustice, and segregation. Today's Jerusalem is tainted by shameful acts of violence and division. Jerusalem is slowly dying. The holy city of peace and love will never exist, at least not in our lifetime.

Jerusalem, the capital city of Israel, has a rich history that dates back to the fourth millennium BC, making it one of the oldest cities in the world. Its population runs close to 750,000 citizens. It is a special place for three of the world's major religions: Judaism, Islam, and Christianity. Jerusalem is the centre of the Jewish faith, and Christians believe Jerusalem to be the land where their savior, Jesus Christ, lived, preached, and was resurrected. And according to Islam, the prophet Mohammed was transported from Mecca to Jerusalem, from where he made his ascent to heaven. Many shrines to each of these religions have been built in the city and destroyed over the centuries.

The Old City sector of Jerusalem is tiny, with an area of less than one square kilometer (0.35 sq mi), and yet some of the most important religious sites can be found there: the Temple Mount, the Western Wall, the Church of the Holy Sepulchre, the Dome of the Rock, and al-Aqsa Mosque. Now protected as a World Heritage Site, the ancient walled city has been destroyed

twice, besieged twenty-three times, attacked fifty-two times, and captured and recaptured forty-four times.

The real bone of contention today is East Jerusalem, which includes the Old City. In 1948, as a result of the Arab-Israeli War, Israel and Jordan conquered different parts of the city. Jordan claimed East Jerusalem, and Israel claimed the rest of the city. It wasn't long before Jordan assumed control of the holy places within the Old City, which was contrary to the terms of their agreement with Israel. They denied Israelis access to their Jewish holy sites, while Christian Israelis were granted limited access. Many of the sites were desecrated, while Muslim sites underwent under significant renovations.

War was imminent. In 1967, Israel captured East Jerusalem during the Six-Day War. Their goal was to assume sovereignty over the entire city. Jews and Christians were once again given access to the area, while the Temple Mount remained under Islamic jurisdiction. Since 1967, Israel has expanded beyond the agreed boundaries. The United Nations declared that Israel's claim over East Jerusalem was a violation of international law.

Human rights	4/10
Violence	6/10
World reach	7/10
Inevitability	7/10
Destruction	4/10
Average score	5.6/10

Left: Policeman in Jerusalem.

Left: Flag of Equatorial Guinea.

Patrick Bonneville: One of the smallest countries in the world, the population of Equatorial Guinea in the 1970s was a mere 300,000. But under the reign of its first president, one third of the population was killed. Then the country collapsed.

In October 1968, a small nation on the west coast of Africa claimed its independence from Spain. The first president of Equatorial Guinea, Francisco Macías Nguema, took only two years to create a one-party state and plunge the country into a reign of terror that killed one-third of the country's small population of 300,000.

In his self-styled cult of personality, he called himself the "Unique Miracle" and "Grand Master of Education, Science, and Culture." He imposed the death penalty, and insulting or offending him or his cabinet meant prison for thirty years. By his own constitutional decree, he was President-for-Life and had absolute power. Among his authoritarian tactics, he ordered all boats in the country destroyed, burned over $105 million dollars in Guinean and foreign currency—about half the cash in the country, killed about 50,000 people

and drove another 150,000 into exile, and forced, at gunpoint, 20,000 citizens into slave work. In one horrific event, he oversaw the public execution of 150 political prisoner's on Christmas Eve as the song "Those Were the Days, My Friend" played over loudspeakers. His reign brought about the failure of the country's main export industry, cocoa.

On August 3, 1979, Macías Nguema's nephew, Teodoro Obiang Nguema Mbasogo, launched a bloody coup d'état. Macías Nguema was placed on trial and was subsequently sentenced to death. He faced his end on September 29, 1979, by firing squad.

Today, Equatorial Guinea has begun to overcome its mountainous debts and sorrows. With the discovery of large oil and gas deposits off its small islands in the Atlantic, its economy is in spectacular growth and it is the most prosperous African nation. Despite the state's riches, however, the country still ranks near the bottom of the UN human development index. The watchdog agency Transparency International, that monitors government corruption, evaluates Equatorial Guinea in the top ten, with current president Obiang claiming oil revenues are state secrets.

Human rights	6/10
Violence	9/10
World reach	3/10
Inevitability	5/10
Destruction	5/10
Average score	5.6/10

Patrick Bonneville: The Kashmir Conflict is another terrible legacy of the British Empire. When the British left the region, troubles blazed.

Jammu and Kashmir is a north-western Indian region that is disputed by Pakistan and China, and the people of Kashmir. India administers about 43 percent of Kashmir, Pakistan about 37 percent, and China about 20 percent. While India claims that the region is "integral" to their union, the Pakistani position is that the Kashmir people themselves should decide their status. Some Kashmir groups want independence from all claims.

The conflict dates from India's independence from Britain in 1947, when the partitioning of the former British colony created two new nations, the Union of India and the Dominion of Pakistan. A total of 565 princely states in the Kashmir region—representing a population of about 99 million—had to decide whether to join India or Pakistan.

Faced by this seemingly impossible decision, the then-ruler of Jammu and Kashmir signed an agreement with Pakistan allowing trade and communications to continue without hindrance. He did not sign an equivalent deal with India. The Indo-Pakistani War of 1947, sometimes known as the First Kashmir War, was fought between India and Pakistan over the region from 1947 to 1948. It was the first of four wars fought between the two newly independent nations—others took place in 1965

Above: Indian soldiers guard the border.

and 1999. India and China also went to war over Kashmir in 1962.

These, and other clashes in the region, have left thousands dead. Many claims of human rights abuses have been made against the Indian Armed Forces, and Médecins Sans Frontières evaluates that Kashmiri women suffer some of the worst sexual violence in the world—over 11 percent of women in the region have reported being victims of rape. It is reasonable to assume that most of the rapes taking place go unreported.

"I just wish India and Pakistan could find a solution once and for all."
—Kashmir resident Anjali, age fourteen, in an interview with the BBC in 2002

Human rights	7/10
Violence	7/10
World reach	5/10
Inevitability	5/10
Destruction	4/10
Average score	5.6/10

Patrick Bonneville: The disappearance of the rainforests means poorer air quality. It means no more habitat for thousands of species. And maybe it will eventually mean no more humans. Why is it so hard to protect the rainforests from ourselves?

Above: Deforestation in Brazil, aerial view of a large soy field eating into the tropical rainforest.

We now know that rainforests play a vital role in the health of the planet. They are home to between 40 and 75 percent of all species on Earth, and scientists believe that there are still millions of rainforest species undiscovered. Rainforests have been called the "jewels of the Earth" and "the world's largest pharmacy." A whopping 28 percent of our oxygen is produced in rainforests, giving rise to another nickname, "the lungs of the Earth."

Rainforests differ from jungles in many ways. They receive an above average annual rainfall—between 68-78 inches (or 1750-2000 mm)—and have a high canopy of leaves that prohibits sunlight from reaching the forest floor. This means that rainforest floors are sparse and walkable. The forests are typically found in the tropics, along the equator.

Humans systematically raze tropical and temperate rainforests. Most biologists estimate that more than 50,000 species become extinct each year because of deforestation. Such a trend could mean the elimination of more than a quarter of all life on Earth within fifty years. Brazil, for example, has lost an incredible 95 percent of its rainforests and has declared the loss a national emergency.

There are some skeptical voices that claim that there is no concrete proof that our rainforests are disappearing. They claim that for every tree cut down, there is another one somewhere, growing to take its place. With such confusion, it is difficult to evaluate the current situation. One reliable tool is satellite imagery: in 2002, satellite photos showed that approximately 5.8 million hectares of tropical rainforests had been leveled. While this figure was 23 percent less than had been estimated, deforestation in the Amazon is growing twice as fast as previously believed. Despite these discrepancies, most experts agree that the destruction of our rainforests is an essential environmental issue that needs to rectified.

Human rights	1/10
Violence	0/10
World reach	7.5/10
Inevitability	9/10
Destruction	10/10
Average score	5.5/10

Patrick Bonneville: If our rainforests are the lungs of the Earth, then our old-growth forests are its mind and memory. I saw a tree in Florida that was 3,000 years old. I saw the redwood that still stands because of John Muir. Where I live, I am surrounded by boreal forest, full of life. I plant over fifty trees on my land every year. Still, I buy furniture from Indonesia and hardwood flooring made in China. I print tens of thousands of books a year.

Above: Devasted forest in Tasmania, Australia.

Deforestation involves the removal of trees in a forested area by logging or burning. People clear forest land for several reasons: to make pastures or crop fields; to harvest wood for the manufacture of wood products or by-products, such as paper; and for the making of charcoal, such as in Haiti. It takes place on nearly every continent. Some environmental groups claim that one-fifth of the world's rainforests were destroyed in a time span of thirty years; if the trend continues unchecked, they might be completely eradicated by 2020. Conservationists worry that a similar fate is in store for our old-growth forests.

People have been destroying old-growth forests for a long time. From 1100 to 1500 AD, there was a ship building boom for which entire forests were destroyed in one go. An estimated 6,000 mature oaks were required to build the British Admiral Horatio Nelson's Royal Navy war ships. Not surprisingly, there was an increase in flooding around the same time. The use of charcoal as a fuel source for heating, cooking, and smelting iron ore in Europe also greatly contributed to the deforestation of that continent.

Deforestation takes a devastating toll on the land and its wildlife. Animal habitats are disturbed and their food sources compromised. Increased soil erosion means increased vulnerability to natural disaster. Regardless of the figures, most experts agree that destruction of forests is a significant problem. The Kyoto Protocol called for the reduction of emissions that result from deforestation and forest degradation by 2008. Only Denmark, Germany, and the United Kingdom succeeded, and they are countries that rely little on the forestry industry. All the other signees increased their emissions from deforestation. China's emissions jumped a whopping 150 percent.

Human rights	0/10
Violence	0/10
World reach	8/10
Inevitability	9/10
Destruction	10/10
Average score	5.4/10

Patrick Bonneville: Recent scars have been added to the old ones in this beautiful Middle Eastern country. I wonder when this region will at last be at peace. How many generations will it take? I hope our children will do better than we did to solve this seemingly eternal conflict.

With the creation of the state of Israel in 1948, the arrival of displaced Palestinian refugees in Lebanon began; they made up about 10 percent of the total population of the country, changing the demographics of Lebanon forever. The new state of Israel also provided a foundation for long-term regional conflict. The fifteen-year Lebanese Civil War started in April 1975 and claimed some 250,000 lives. It left more than 1,000,000 people injured, many of them crippled for the rest of their lives.

A mix of religious differences, ethnicities, border skirmishes, and deep-rooted hatred created tensions between neighbors Israel and Lebanon and between the Palestinians and their Lebanese hosts. These tensions increased steadily for much of the mid-1900s. In 1967, the southern region of the country became the arena for fighting between Israeli and Palestinian commandos and was completely devastated. Tensions between Israel and Syria were also strongly boiling during that period, with Lebanon stuck in the middle.

In the spring of 1975, Lebanon exploded. Politicians were murdered, members of opposing groups were killed, and militias took control of small regions. Roads were blocked and citizens executed without warning. The population was divided; Palestinians and Lebanese were at loggerheads, and Beirut was falling apart.

In 1982, Israel decided to take over. They invaded the country, and Beirut, the center of the invasion, lost thousands of civilians. One of the worst events of this period was the Sabra and Shatila refugee camp massacres. In September 1982, a Christian Lebanese militia group entered two of these refugee camps, under Israeli supervision, and coldly killed Palestinian and Lebanese Muslim civilians. It was said to be a reprisal for massacres committed by Islamic Palestine Liberation Organization (PLO) units a few years earlier.

In late 1989 and early 1990, the unrest came to end with the help of the Arab League. In 2006, however, the painful scar was re-opened when the Lebanon-based Islamic paramilitary group Hezbollah attacked Israeli forces, prompting Israel to respond with heavy military gear.

Human rights	7/10
Violence	7/10
World reach	2/10
Inevitability	5/10
Destruction	6/10
Average score	5.4/10

Right: Damage to the Holiday Inn in Beirut.

According to the World Wildlife Fund (WWF), wildlife trade is the practice of selling or exchanging non-domesticated animals and plant resources. It is wholly consumer-driven. TRAFFIC, the monitoring network for the WWF and the World Conservation Union (IUCN), estimates legal wildlife trade to be worth around $160 billion. WWF has documented that there were over 100 million tonnes of fish, 1.5 million live birds, and 440,000 tonnes of medicinal plants traded in just one year.

It is virtually impossible to estimate the worth of this illegal activity. What is known, however, is that because illegal harvesters and poachers do not heed conservation laws, their practices entail environmental destruction, species extinction, habitat deterioration, population decreases, and disruption to the food chain. At the top of the food chain, of course, is humanity. The overexploitation of some species affects our well-being, too. If, for example, a certain species of plant disappears, the animal who feeds on it might migrate or, eventually, die out. Humans that hunted that animal for meat can no longer do so, and their easiest-to-access food source is gone. In another example, the introduction of non-native plants and animals to a region can destroy its natural balance.

Some "wildlife trade hotspots" include China's international borders, certain regions of East and Southern Africa, Southeast Asia, the Eastern European Union, parts of Mexico, the Caribbean, Indonesia, as well as New Guinea and the Solomon Islands.

The international trade of many species is regulated by the Convention on International Trade in Endangered Species of Wild Fauna and Flora (CITES). There are also organizations that lobby governments for improved laws and regulations for the conservation of species and restrictions on trade. The great challenge remains to educate poachers and traders, who themselves are often from very poor regions, about the laws and effects regarding trading. Perhaps the most essential element in stopping the illegal trade of wildlife is change in consumer behavior and the creation of laws banning the retail sale of such plant and animal-derived products.

Above: Illegal wildlife trade exists because there is a strong demand for the animals around the world.

Human rights	0/10
Violence	2/10
World reach	9/10
Inevitability	8/10
Destruction	7/10
Average score	5.2/10

Patrick Bonneville: It is as though humankind is God on earth, and all other species are doomed to extinction.

A spectacular example of humanity's disruption of nature is the extinction of Raphus cucullatus. Otherwise known as the dodo bird, this native to Mauritius was a flightless bird with no real predators. When humans arrived on the island in the late 1500s, the cats, dogs, and pigs they brought made short work of the one meter (three feet) high bird that couldn't fly away. It is also surmised that people also destroyed their nesting grounds, if not their nests. Within eighty years of the arrival of people in Mauritius, the bird was extinct.

Today, the International Union for the Conservation of Nature (IUCN) monitors the vulnerability to extinction of all animals known to be at risk. Their Red List suggests that at least 1,141 of the 5,487 mammals on our planet are threatened. They have catalogued the extinction of at least seventy-six mammals since 1500. The IUCN also conducts research related to the conservation and recovery of such animals.

Animal extinction is intricately related to the viability of the food chain. The Iberian lynx, for example, has an adult population of under one hundred because its primary source of food, the European rabbit, is in decline.

Some species have been brought back from the brink of extinction through conservation efforts in the wild or in

Above: The tiger is an endangered species.

zoos. The Père David's deer, once native to China, was hunted nearly to extinction. A few remaining deer were sent to zoos around the world, where they have bred successfully. There has been some luck in reintroducing them to the wild.

Another threat to wildlife is disease. Cancer in animals has increased and seems to kill wild animals at similar rates as it does humans. It is likely that this is a result of environmental pollution; where rivers, lakes, and oceans have become increasingly contaminated with toxic waste and other kinds of pollution, increases in cancerous tumors have been documented. Only through changes in human behavior can this pattern be changed.

"I really care that so many species have been wiped out, like genocide of entire races."
—Leonardo DiCaprio

Human rights	0/10
Violence	6/10
World reach	10/10
Inevitability	8/10
Destruction	2/10
Average score	5.2/10

Forced marriage implies the lack of consent of either one or both individuals to the contract. Often, false consent is obtained, or one or both parties agree to the marriage out of fear of violence, physical abuse, psychological or emotional manipulation, or even death.

Forced marriages should not be confused with arranged marriages. In the cultural practice of arranged marriages, the parents choose a spouse for their child. The couple generally meet only briefly or not at all before the ceremony. In medieval times, in the West, the practice was popular among royalty to ensure royal bloodlines and cement political ties between countries.

Victims of forced marriages can be women, men, and even children—there are documented cases of families selling a child into marriage as a way of providing for their other children. A forced marriage may be used as a means of gaining entry as an immigrant into a specific country or as the payback of a family debt. A person may also be forced into a marriage in order to secure a dowry, or in order to bind two tribes together. In this case it is, essentially, a political act.

One form of forced marriage is known as bride kidnapping, in which a woman is taken from her home by force and secretly wed to the kidnapper. This practice was once widespread and still occurs today in parts of Asia, Africa, Mexico, and among the Romani people. The act generally serves a political purpose.

Many countries have laws prohibiting the practice. The United Kingdom enacted a law in 2007 that gives legal protection to the victims, if they ask for it. But in most countries where the practice is prevalent, little is done to prevent it.

"No marriage shall be legally entered into without the full and free consent of both parties, such consent to be expressed by them in person after due publicity and in the presence of the authority competent to solemnize the marriage and of witnesses, as prescribed by law."
—Office of the United Nations' High Commissioner for Human Rights.

Human rights	10/10
Violence	3/10
World reach	5/10
Inevitability	8/10
Destruction	0/10
Average score	5.2/10

Above: Traditional Indian bride.

Press restrictions in Russia mean that the mass media is unable to independently report on government policy; they also limit access to information by journalists. Mass media includes television, radio, periodicals and the Internet, whether state-run or private. Reporters without Borders ranks Russia near the bottom in the World Press Freedom Index, at 144 out of 169, and describes Russia as the third deadliest country for reporters between 1992 and 2006.

The recent death of the Russian journalist and human rights activist Anna Politkovskaya enraged the international community. An outspoken critic of Russia's policies towards Chechnya, she was shot in the lobby of her apartment building. The KGB's director has commented that this murder, as well as that of investigative journalist Yuri Shchekochikhin, is proof of Russian-sanctioned political assassinations.

Internet users enjoy relative freedom; Russia was not listed on Reporters without Borders' list of the twelve "Enemies of the Internet" in 2009. Nevertheless, in August of 2008, the editor of the website Ingushetia.org, Magomed Yevloyev, was murdered while in police custody. His website was critical of administration policies in Ingushetia, a poor and troubled region of Russia. Human rights groups were outraged by his death and the U.S. State Department called for an investigation. The Russian government agreed, all the while maintaining their official stance that Yevloyev was shot for resisting arrest. In fact, in 2008, Human Rights Watch documented dozens of arbitrary detentions, disappearances, torture, and extra-judicial executions in Ingushetia.

There have been many other suspicious murders: Vladislav Nikolayevich Listyev was shot in 1995. Iskandar Khatloni was axed in the head in 2000. He was covering human rights abuses in Chechnya.

The list goes on. Journalist Yuri Petrovich Shchekochikhin died in 2003. Paul Klebnikov was shot in 2004. Ivan Ivanovich Safronov died in 2007. Journalist Abdulla Telman Alishayev was shot in 2008.

Above: The third anniversary of the death of Russian journalist Anna Politkovskaya. She was assassinated in the elevator of her apartment building in 2006. The case remains unsolved.

Human rights	7/10
Violence	5/10
World reach	6/10
Inevitability	8/10
Destruction	0/10
Average score	5.2/10

The Union of Myanmar is most commonly known in the West as Burma. Located in Asia, it shares borders with China, Thailand, Bangladesh, India, the Bay of Bengal, Laos, and the Andaman Sea. The State Peace and Development Council is the country's military arm that seized power in 1988. It is responsible for persistent human rights abuses in Myanmar, including the house arrest of the democratically elected leader, Aung San Suu Kyi.

Once the world's largest exporters of rice, while under British rule the country was the wealthiest in Southeast Asia. Since the 1962 coup d'etat, however, Myanmar has spiralled into economic catastrophy. Its 56 million residents now belong to one of the most impoverished countries on the planet.

The current government is a military junta, or a committee of military leaders. It is firmly non-democratic. The government's role in the aftermath of 2008's Cyclone Nargis caused much suffering for its people. On May 3, the cyclone blasted through a densely populated region of Myanmar, with winds reaching 215 kilometers per hour (135 mph). It wiped out entire villages. More than 200,000 people were killed or reported missing, and damages were evaluated at $10 billion. The United Nations estimated that one million people were left homeless and the World Health Organization reported severe outbreaks of malaria. It was the worst natural disaster in Burmese recorded history.

There are some skeptical voices that, to the frustration of the international community, the Burmese government complicated international relief efforts. Although the UN had organized relief planes of food, medicine and other supplies, the government denied visas to aid organizations. When India offered help, however, the government opened its doors. It is estimated that two weeks after the cyclone, only 25 percent of people in need of aid actually received any. The delays provoked international condemnation, and foreign journalists were compelled to flee the country for fear of imprisonment.

The UN had urged Burma to accept aid "without hindrance," especially since a second storm was on its way. Oxfam International issued a warning that millions would die if clean water and proper sanitation resources were not immediately installed. Myanmar, however, was either ignorant of the true situation or too entrenched in its isolationism to accept the aid its people so deperately needed. Some critics have gone as far as suggesting that the Myanmar government was opportunistic and used the disaster as a means of genocide.

"We are in a long line of nations who are ready, willing, and able to help, but also, of course, in a long line of nations the Burmese don't trust. It's more than frustrating. It's a tragedy."
—U.S. ambassador Eric John, in Bangkok

Right: A mother and her two daughters receive blankets distributed by UNHCR to the survivors of Cyclone Nargis.

Human rights	7.5/10
Violence	2/10
World reach	4/10
Inevitability	10/10
Destruction	2/10
Average score	5.1/10

Patrick Bonneville: Ethiopia, the only un-colonized country in Africa, has a very long agricultural history. The whole economy of Ethiopia is based on its harvest, and in 1984 and 1985, when insurgent groups became more active in Northern and the Southern Ethiopia, the country's agriculture collapsed. So did the country. Millions of people perished because of the famines.

A confluence of sad events led to the terrible famines of 1984 and '85. Lack of rainfall, the political rebellion, and the government's counterinsurgency measures led the country into two years of famine. In the Northern regions, the People's Liberation Front played a role, and in the South, the Oromo Liberation Front insurgency compounded drought and caused over one million people to starve to death. Ethiopia had also experienced two major droughts in the late 1970s. The presence of war this time, however, meant that the government was ill-prepared to deal with a hungry population. About eight million Ethiopians overall fell victim to the famine.

In 1984, the BBC first documented the famine, with journalist Michael Buerk describing it as "a biblical famine in the twentieth century." The crisis awoke the sympathies of the whole world.

After the BBC broadcast, the Royal Air Force began their aid efforts with help from Germany, Poland, Canada, the USA, and the Soviet Union. British musician Bob Geldolf organized the "Live Aid" event, which 400 million viewers from over sixty countries watched on TV. Live Aid raised about $2.5 million.

Paradoxically, at least one scholar, famine expert Alex de Waal, has declared that the humanitarian efforts actually prolonged the war, and as a result, prolonged human suffering.

"Twenty years ago, when we saw an equally terrible situation in Ethiopia, we swore this can't happen again and it's happening. We have been unable to ameliorate what is probably the most severe food crisis anywhere in the world."
—Ken Hackett, president of Catholic Relief Services

"We give birth to the children but we can't grow them."
—Urmale Kasaso, a young Ethiopian mother in an interview with USA Today

Left: Severely malnourished drought victim at a relief camp in Korem, in the heart of one of the worst-affected areas of Ethiopia.

Human rights	7/10
Violence	2/10
World reach	2/10
Inevitability	9/10
Destruction	5/10
Average score	5.0/10

Patrick Bonneville: This illness could easily be eradicated from the Earth. How? Just transfer a few dollars from all defense budgets to the cause. Give it to the UN's World Health Organization and its partners. It might be a better investment. The WHO has documentation proving that malaria can be reduced: the Maldives, Tunisia, and the United Arab Emirates have all eliminated the disease. Malaria is preventable and curable.

When a Westerner wants to travel to tropical countries, the travel agent will suggest protection against malaria. If such protection is available, why do an estimated one to three million people die each year from the disease? Common in tropical and subtropical regions worldwide, approximately 350 to 500 million new cases are reported annually. Most deaths from malaria occur in Sub-Saharan Africa.

Malaria is a vector-borne infectious disease that is typically caused by the bite of a female anopheles mosquito infected with microscopic parasites. Only anopheles mosquitoes transmit the disease. In some cases, the infection leads to death, especially among children who have not had time to develop a natural resistance to the disease. Although malaria is known to have existed for over 50,000 years, it was only in the early 1900s that scientists discovered how the disease was transmitted.

Malaria's effect on the human population is devastating. In Africa alone, there are an estimated 89.6 million children living unprotected in areas prone to the disease. One simple and inexpensive form of protection is a mosquito net draped over the bed, since anopheles mosquitoes bite at night. Some humanitarian programs distribute insecticide-impregnated nets. The World Heath Organization has included these nets, which can cost as little as $2.50, in its Millennium Development Goals. The nets, however, are often not distributed, and people trade them instead for much-needed cash or food. Others use the nets for fishing. Clearly, impoverished people are too often forced to weigh the risk of malaria against the risk of not eating.

Pharmaceutical companies have developed drugs for those who have become infected. If a treated person is once again bitten by a mosquito, though, the insect will ingest a tiny bit of the pharmaceutical and its malarial parasites can mutate to develop a resistance to the drug. In fact, the WHO calls antimalarial drug resistance a major public health problem.

Antimalarial drugs are also expensive. The best hope for the future is the continued use of preventative drugs. In 2002, the public/private partnership Global Fund to Fight AIDS, Tuberculosis and Malaria was initiated. Over 1.9 million lives have been saved thanks to the efforts of this fund.

"Malaria is preventable and curable."
—World Health Organization

Right: The female mosquito transmits the disease to humans.

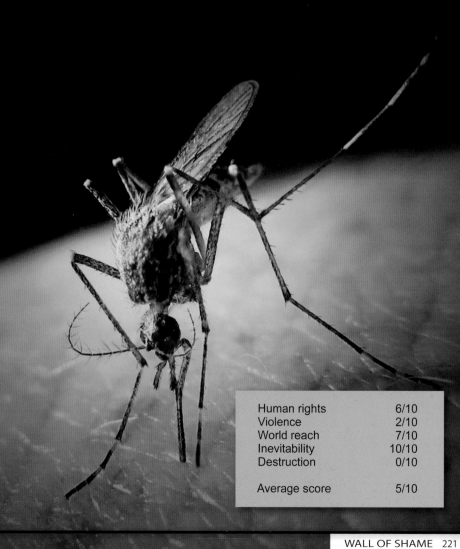

Human rights	6/10
Violence	2/10
World reach	7/10
Inevitability	10/10
Destruction	0/10
Average score	5/10

The Republic of Colombia joins South America to Central America and touches both the Atlantic and Pacific oceans. It is the third most populous country in Latin America, with an estimated 44.6 million inhabitants.

Colombia has been in a state of civil war for about forty-five years. The Revolutionary Armed Forces of Colombia (FARC) and the National Liberation Army (ELN) have both been active in guerrilla warfare aimed at destroying various government administrations. The assassination of political leader Jorge Eliécer Gaitán in 1964 and the subsequent killing of about 400 people were the genesis of the conflict. In the midst of the ongoing political instability in Colombia, the illegal drug trade has flourished. The manufacture and export of cocaine have pushed the country into such violence that very few other countries know. Colombians are no strangers to mysterious "disappearances," kidnappings, massacres, torture, and assassinations. Children are forcibly recruited into paramilitary organizations. Since the beginning of the civil war, over three million people have been displaced, often ending up in slums with little access to health services or education.

Born of two highly segregated societies, Colombia is home to rich upper-class families of Spanish descent and the majority mestizo, or those of mixed native South-American and Spanish ancestry. For many, a way out of the slums is through the drug trade. Government, left-wing insurgents, and right-wing paramilitary organizations have all been accused of having their hands in this pot.

In 2007, violent crime and kidnapping were the lowest they have been in twenty years. Thousands of paramilitary soldiers have turned in their weapons as a gesture of peace, and international experts say that rebel forces have been weakened. Progress remains slow, however; and there is little hope for prosecution of those responsible for human rights violations.

"We need to fight for the freedom of the others, who are still in the jungle, still held by FARC. There are a lot of people around the world who want to help us—fighting for the liberty of other Colombians." —Ingrid Betancourt, held hostage by a paramilitary organization

Human rights	6/10
Violence	8/10
World reach	5/10
Inevitability	4/10
Destruction	2/10
Average score	5.0/10

Left: Colombia produces 90% of the cocaine in the world.

Patrick Bonneville: It is shameful that Indian and Nepalese authorities, as well as the parents of these girls, failed to protect their daughters.

Tulasa Thapa was born in 1970 in a small village near Kathmandu, Nepal. When she was twelve years old, she was kidnapped and sold into prostitution in Mumbai. She was repeatedly beaten and raped in preparation for her future in the sex trade, which would unfold in three different brothels. She was obligated to have sex with at least three clients each night, although it might have been as many as eight. One hotel manager reported her to the police in 1985, when she was fifteen. At that time, she was suffering from three types of sexually transmitted diseases, genital warts, and brain tuberculosis. She spent the rest of her life in a wheelchair, until her death in 1995, from tuberculosis. The governments of India and Nepal signed a treaty after Tulasa's death vowing to free Nepali girls from this industry.

Tulasa's life mirrors those of hundreds of thousands of women and children forcibly employed in brothels and prostitution. Human Rights Watch asserts that in India's Mumbai alone, there an estimated 100,000 forced sex workers. About 40 percent of them are from Nepal, and 20 percent of them are under eighteen years old. At least half the workers are infected with HIV. Escape for these women and children seems impossible: they are threatened with harm and are under constant surveillance.

Above: Young girls are recruited in isolated villages in Nepal.

The Nepali families of these young girls are often indebted or hungry. Daughters are sold for a pittance into the sex trade to settle debts or to relieve families of a mouth to feed—a girl might be sold for as little as $4. Border guards are bribed into letting the girls through into India.

Although Nepal and India both have laws against human trafficking and the sex-trade, very little is done to enforce them. International scrutiny and pressure fall on deaf ears. Extreme poverty in both countries makes human trafficking very profitable. For this shameful trade, issues of poverty must be addressed before the sex-slave industry can be suppressed. Despite economic improvements at the national level, positive effects are not reaching the rural communities

Human rights	8/10
Violence	8/10
World reach	2/10
Inevitability	7/10
Destruction	0/10
Average score	5.0/10

The Greek Civil War came fast on the heels of World War II. Upon the withdrawal of German troops, the British established control in Greece. In 1944, two Greek guerrilla forces set up bases in the Greek mountains with the goal of taking control of the country. They were the communist-controlled National Liberation Front-National Popular Liberation Army (EAM-ELAS) and the Greek Democratic National Army (EDES). It was only a matter of weeks before the guerrilla groups controlled all of Greece, with the exception of Athens and Salonika.

Greece would live with civil war until 1949. The guerillas' first attempt at control ended in a defeat for the communist rebel forces in 1945, followed by a general election in March of 1946. When the king returned to the throne following the election, the rebels regrouped and within a year proclaimed a provisional government in the northern mountains. With U.S.-backed military support, the Greek army succeeded in expelling the communist rebels from their territories; the rebels fled to Albania. During the three-year conflict, an estimated 50,000 soldiers died, and some reports estimate that between 500,000 and one million Greeks were forced from their homes in order to escape the fighting.

Since 1949, there have been continued isolated attempts at communist control. Although Greece was accepted into NATO at the end of the civil war, the country was left in ruins physically, emotionally, and financially; the civil war caused devastation that lasted for decades.

A recent poll suggests that nearly half the Greek population still is unsure as to the success of the war: of those polled, only 43 percent felt it was a good thing that the right had won, while a significant 24 percent did not respond.

"This is history. I can't believe it. Greece, my birthplace Greece, the land of my ancestors. I've longed for this moment, I've dreamed about it for 55 entire years."
—Georgi Donevski, refugee getting back his Greek citizenship in 2003

Human rights	7/10
Violence	6/10
World reach	2/10
Inevitability	5/10
Destruction	5/10
Average score	5.0/10

Left: Thousands of Greek children were evacuated during the Civil War. Many never returned.

The United Nations World Tourism Organization (UNWTO) defines sex tourism as "trips organized from within the tourism sector, or from outside this sector but using its structures and networks, with the primary purpose of effecting a commercial sexual relationship by the tourist with residents at the destination."

Above: Thailand is still a very popular destination.

Many sex tourists travel from the West to indulge in sex acts that are not condoned at home or in order to escape scrutiny by police and peers. The business sex tourists patronize can involve adult prostitution, child prostitution, and forced prostitution. While sex tourism with adult prostitutes may be morally questionable, it can be consensual—at the very least, it reflects the economic desperation of women prostitutes around the world. More serious, however, are the implications of child prostitution and forced prostitution.

Child sex tourism refers to the act of visiting a foreign territory with the intention of paying for sexual activities with a minor. There are several countries where this practice is more prevalent than others, such as Thailand, Cambodia, India, Brazil, and Mexico. An estimated two million children are believed to be victims of this multi-billion dollar industry.

"The incredible escalation of child prostitution ... is directly caused by the tourist trade. Child prostitution is the newest tourist attraction offered by developing countries."
—Interpol

While there are laws that are intended to quash the industry, sex tourism is inherently linked to poverty; the financial rewards keep the business alive. There are reports of families selling their children into the industry as a way to get money. Some reports cite children as young as five years old being used as sex slaves. Since it is most commonly a taboo subject for families to reveal such pacts with procurers, the real extent of this kind of dealing may never be known.

Several larger issues need to be addressed before sex tourism can ever be stopped. Poverty, education, human rights, and criminal activities are deeply interwoven with sex tourism. Until the real causes of poverty and sexual compulsions are addressed, the end of sex tourism and may be far down the road.

Human rights	8/10
Violence	3/10
World reach	7/10
Inevitability	7/10
Destruction	0/10
Average score	5.0/10

Mediterranean Sea

Cyprus

Mediterranean Sea

Because of its strategic location in the Eastern Mediterranean Sea, the island of Cyprus has been desired as a geopolitical asset by many nations and empires. Its known history dates back to the tenth millennium BC. In the twentieth century, possession of the island was disputed by Turkey and Greece, the two neighboring countries who have peopled the island over time. Today, a military division separates Turkish Cypriots from Greek Cypriots, who represent three-quarters of the island's population.

In 1960, an agreement was signed between the United Kingdom, Greece, and Turkey for the independence of the island from the United Kingdom, which had managed the island since 1878. Greek and Turkish Cypriots failed to put in place a working government, and arguments and violence between the two communities persisted until the end of 1963, when a United Nations peacekeeping mission was sent to the island. It has never left.

On July 20, 1974, at the request of Turkish Cypriot leaders, Turkey launched an attack on the northern sector of the island. The invasion meant a gain of one third of Cyprus for the Turks and led to the division of the country into two distinct regions, the Turkish side and the Greek side. The line separating the two would become known as the Attila Line. Greek Cypriots stuck on the Turkish side became "refugees" and were forced to leave their homes to seek refuge on the Greek side. They represented more than 80 percent of the population in the now-Turkish Cyprus. Turks from the mainland were invited to take their place.

In 1983, the United Nations declared the Turkish Republic of Northern Cyprus invalid and asked for a withdrawal. This was ignored by Turkey. In 2004, the two communities of the island were asked by a United Nations-sponsored referendum to unite. Turkish Cypriots agreed, and Greek Cypriots refused. The island remains virtually cut in half today.

Above: Political map of Cyprus with its divisions.
Right: Casualities in Santalaris, a small village of the Turkish Republic of Northern Cyprus.
Opposite page: Division of the island.

Human rights   5/10
Violence   7/10
World reach   3/10
Inevitability   8/10
Destruction   2/10

Average score   5.0/10

The Romany or Roma, often referred to in Western society as gypsies, are believed to have migrated from India into eastern and southern Europe in the medieval age. By the sixteenth century, they had migrated as far as England and Russia, and eventually to the New World. They have been both romanticized and demonized in film and literature, where they have been depicted as lovers and entertainers, and conniving manipulators and petty criminals. In reality, they have known great persecution and even genocide.

It is estimated today that there are between nine and fourteen million Romani in the world who speak several dialects of the Romani language. Many groups adopted the language and religion of the country to which they migrated.

Because of their nomadic lifestyle, traditional Romani are mostly uneducated and practice easily mobile trades. Their way of life has often caused them to be perceived as con artists, thieves, and liars. Romani are usually forced into slum neighborhoods and are refused adequate employment and education. They are also often victims of police abuse. In many countries, they are subject to systemic and personal hostility and prejudice, which is called "antiziganism." This is especially present in Bulgaria, Slovakia, Hungary, Slovenia, and Kosovo. Roma children are segregated in the school systems; forced sterilization has been a common practice, and health care is almost non-existent for them.

Left: Romani elder.

Prejudice against the Romani also occurs in the Czech Republic, where 90 percent of Czech people refuse to live next to the Romani. In Kosovo, Romani were forced into refugee communities. In 2007, three Roma women in Slovakia successfully sued a hospital for performing forced sterilizations on them while they were minors and without consent. Italy has proceeded with plans to fingerprint all Romani people in the country. The United Nations responded by declaring that this action would be unambiguously discriminatory, and the European Parliament requested that Italy put an end to the project, calling it a pure and obvious example of discrimination.

It is nearly impossible to list all the examples of systemic racism faced by this ethnic group. Current discrimination claims exist in England, Northern Ireland, Denmark, Norway, and in the United States. It is estimated that during World War II, between 220,000 and 500,000 Romani were murdered by Hitler's Nazi regime. The U.S. Holocaust Memorial Research Institute claims the number may have been as high as 1,500,000.

Human rights	9.5/10
Violence	2/10
World reach	4/10
Inevitability	8/10
Destruction	1/10
Average score	4.9/10

MINA ANTI-PERSONAL PRB M35

Fabricación: BELGA (BEL)

Peso Total: 0.250 Kg.

82 - WESTERN SAHARA

Half a million people live between the Sahara desert and the Atlantic Ocean in a region known as Western Sahara. The area covers 266,000 square kilometers (103,000 square miles). For years, this former Spanish colony has desired independence from its northern neighbor Morocco, which has occupied the area since 1975. The territory dispute has led to a lasting armed conflict that has mainly affected the small population of Western Sahara.

Known before 1975 as Spanish Sahara, the region was annexed by Morocco after the death of Spanish dictator Francisco Franco; Spanish forces completely pulled out of Western Sahara in 1976. Mauritania, located just to the south, had ambitions for the territory but backed away from their claims in 1979.

The local population, the Sahrawi, were already fighting for the independence of Western Sahara from Spanish colonial rule, and they have not given up against the forces of Morocco. The Polisario, the Western Sahara liberation movement, has denounced terrorism and attacks on civilians. Nevertheless, in order to keep the Polisario out of

Opposite page: Western Sahara has been flooded with anti-personnel mines since the beginning of the conflict.
Above: Smiling children in Dakhla refugee camp.

Moroccan-controlled areas of Western Sahara, Morocco built a sand wall, sometimes known as the Wall of Shame. It is 2,700 kilometers long (1,678 miles) and is well protected by soldiers and land mines.

"The international community is called upon to deploy all the political tools necessary in order to make sure that the media, the organizations of defence of the human rights and international observers can reach Western Sahara freely."
—Daha Rahmouni, member of the Sahrawi Association of Victims of Grave Human Rights Violations Committed by the Moroccan State

Human rights	9/10
Violence	5/10
World reach	2/10
Inevitability	6/10
Destruction	2/10
Average score	4.8/10

In the fall of 1968, Mexico City was preparing for the Summer Olympics due to begin in less than two weeks. The events of October 2 began with a peaceful rally at the Plaza de las Tres Culturas, attended by about 10,000 students. They were assembled to protest the government's actions and chanted, "We don't want Olympic Games, we want revolution!" The military brought in about 5,000 soldiers, 200 tanks, and trucks to surround the plaza.

Above: The Mexican army at the Zócalo Square in Mexico City, 1968.

The *Noche de Tlatelolco,* or "Night of Tlatelolco" began at sunset, when shots were fired. The Mexican government maintained for years that shots from the surrounding apartments triggered the army's attack. The student protesters claimed that helicopters overhead signaled the army to begin firing into the crowd. By all accounts, when flares were sent up, the crowd panicked and chaos erupted.

Captain Ernesto Morales Soto claimed that the soldiers were ordered to block exits and prevent people from leaving the plaza. Government troops fired on the demonstrators, killing at least 28 people, although the New York Times reported that as many as 300 were killed and more than 1,000 injured. The killing continued into the night, and witnesses claim that the military simply threw bodies into trucks without even checking to confirm whether they were dead or simply injured.

The event was seemingly swept under the carpet in time for the Summer Games, which began just ten days later and ended without incident.

"I went back early the following morning and saw piles of belts and shoes. Pools of blood remained on the ground despite obvious efforts to wash them away. I also saw large bullet holes on concrete pillars at adult head height."
—*Javier Zúñiga, witness of the massacre*

Human rights	7/10
Violence	8/10
World reach	1/10
Inevitability	6/10
Destruction	2/10
Average score	4.8/10

Left: When the old center of Hama was destroyed by bombs and tanks, thousands of civilians were killed.

On February 2, 1982, in the city of Hama, Syria, the army launched an attack to against the fundamentalist Muslim Brotherhood. The Syrian Human Rights Committee estimates that as many as 40,000 people were killed, including about 1,000 soldiers. The city of Hama was destroyed, including palaces, mosques, ancient ruins, and the famous Azem Palace mansion.

As with many stories of the Middle East, the context of this massacre is complicated. Hama was a stronghold for the Muslim Brotherhood, a radical islamist group that was at loggerheads with the Ba'thist Syrian government, under the leadership of Hafez al-Assad. The government launched abusive attacks on the Muslim Brotherhood and issued a law making membership in the organization a capital offense. As a result, the Brotherhood staged several bomb attacks against the government and government officials, including

an assassination attempt on President Hafez al-Assad. Al-Assad survived and, in revenge, had about 1,000 Islamist prisoners murdered in their cells in Tadmor Prison.

As the Brotherhood called for further retaliation, the government advanced on Hama. Al-Assad called for the city's surrender and then proceeded to bombard it from the air, crush its people's homes, and pump poison gases into its buildings. The attack was followed by several weeks of torture and mass executions of rebel sympathizers.

"Preceding the massacre, the regime started to provoke practices against the citizens by killing, arresting, bombing houses, and abusing the children, women, and elderly. This was the spark that lead to the ignition of the bloodshed."
—*Syrian Human Rights Committee*

Human rights	7/10
Violence	8/10
World reach	1/10
Inevitability	6/10
Destruction	2/10
Average score	4.8/10

Patrick Bonneville: In the winter of 1992, many wonderful things were happening around the world. In one troubled region, however, eighty-three children were shot dead, along with their parents and neighbors. They weren't at the wrong place at the wrong time, they were the wrong ethnicity.

From February 1988 to May 1994, south-western Azerbaijan was the scene of a violent armed conflict. The Nagorno-Karabakh War was an ethnic war between the Republic of Azerbaijan and the ethnic Armenian majority, supported by the neighboring Republic of Armenia. On February 25, 1992, in the town of Khojaly, hundreds of ethnic Azerbaijani residents were killed during a massacre orchestrated by ethnic Armenian forces and backed by the Russian 366th Motor Rifle Regiment. The official death toll is shocking: 613 civilians, including 106 women and 83 children.

Human Rights Watch claimed that the Armenian military ruthlessly opened fire upon Azerbaijani civilians as they were trying to leave the city. Armenian sources maintained that the killings were a result of wartime operations. From a humanitarian standpoint, the vast killing of innocent civilians is not a result of war, it is a result of genocide.

Human Rights Watch calls the Khojaly Massacre the largest massacre to date in the Nagorno-Karabakh conflict. Although the international community called for the Armenians to admit their genocide against the Azerbaijani community, to date, no one has accepted responsibility for the events.

"When we entered the forest of Ketik, we found ourselves under siege by the Armenians. I saw from the bushes how they shot my husband Shura Tapdig oglu Pashayev and my son Elshad Shura oglu Pashayev."
—Kubra Adil qizi Pashayeva, survivor

Above: Murdered Azerbaijani children in the Khojali Massacre.

Human rights	7/10
Violence	8/10
World reach	1/10
Inevitability	6/10
Destruction	2/10
Average score	4.8/10

Atrocities committed against the citizenry included "death flights," in which prisoners were pushed, alive, from planes flying over the Atlantic Ocean or the Rio de la Plata. The newborn babies of female prisoners were taken away and sometimes raised by military men and their families. Torture and illegal firing-squad executions were also rampant.

Argentina's *Guerra Sucia,* "Dirty War," was a prolonged assault on the human rights of its citizens, especially activists and students with left-wing, trade unionist, or revolutionary convictions. Beginning in the 1960s and continuing throughout the war itself, which lasted from 1976 to 1983, an estimated 300,000 people died. The military dictatorship, led by Jorge Rafael Videla, was known to kidnap people in the middle of the night—some of them opponents of the government, others simply "suspect" citizens. They were detained and tortured in secret detention centres and eventually killed. They are known as *los desaparecidos,* or "the disappeared."

The origins of the Dirty War can be traced back to 1973, when clashes between left- and right-wing groups reached a head. In 1974, controversial President Juan Perón died after a series of heart attacks and his wife and vice president, Isabel Perón, assumed power. A military junta led a coup against her and removed her from office. In what they called the "National Reorganization Process," the military government maintained its grip on power by cracking down on anybody they believed was challenging their authority.

The end of a series of military dictatorships was brought about by Argentina's involvement in the Falklands War against the United Kingdom, which had administered the Falkland Islands since 1820. Argentina lost the short war, which it had hoped would rally the Argentinian people around its government. International criticism was mounting, the last of the military juntas failed, and soon allegations of corruption and crimes against humanity were raised. In 1982, Argentina restored basic civil liberties to its citizens and reinstated a political party system. In 1983, the Dirty War ended with Raul Alfonsin's civilian government gaining control. The Argentinian court system would conclude that the previous governments were guilty of committing crimes against humanity.

Human rights	7/10
Violence	7/10
World reach	3/10
Inevitability	6/10
Destruction	1/10
Average score	4.6/10

El bloqueo, "the blockade," is a commercial, economic, and financial embargo imposed on Cuba by the United States in October of 1960. The embargo was passed into law in 1992 as the Cuban Democracy Act, under the pretext that economic sanctions against the country would force the Castro dictatorship to move toward democracy and rethink its views on human rights. In 1996, the U.S. Congress passed a second law, the Helms-Burton Act, that restricts American citizens from doing business in or with Cuba. In 1999, President Bill Clinton modified the act to allow some trade.

Before 1960, the USA had already enforced an arms embargo against Cuba in light of the conflict between Cuban rebels and the country's American-backed leader, Fulgencio Batista. The dictator Batista, however, was overthrown during Fidel Castro's Cuban Revolution of 1959. To reinforce its stance against the rebels, the USA reduced its imports of brown sugar by seven million tons. The Soviet Union jumped in and agreed to purchase the sugar. This move, committed at the height of the Cold War period, confirmed a Cuban alignment with the Soviet Union. President John F. Kennedy then extended the sanctions against the island nation—but not before stocking up on his supply of Cuban cigars, or so the story goes. Tensions rose and by mid-1963, Cuban assets in the United States were frozen.

The current American President, Barack Obama, has a different opinion on the laws and sanctions against Cuba. This, along with the retirement of Fidel Castro and the new Cuban administration under Raúl Castro, lead some to see a glimmer of hope that the relationship between the two countries will improve. The first proof of this was on April 13, 2009, when President Obama revised the travel ban to Cuba, allowing Cuban-Americans to freely travel there. He has also proposed a series of steps for Cuba to follow to prove its openness to change. These steps include releasing political prisoners, allowing American telecommunications companies to operate on the island, and putting an end to the taxation of money sent to Cubans by expatriated relatives living abroad.

The international community has also taken issue with Cuba itself for human rights abuses over the years. Castro's government relentlessly jailed anyone who appeared opposed to his dictatorship. Cuba has also ranked near the very bottom of a long list of countries that deprive citizens of certain freedoms. In the Press Freedom Index of 2008, Reporters Without Borders showed that Cuba has the second-biggest prison in the world for journalists, after the People's Republic of China. Another freedom-depriving law in Cuba means there is a five-year prison term for illegally connecting to the Internet—only a select few Cubans are allowed Internet access, and they are closely monitored.

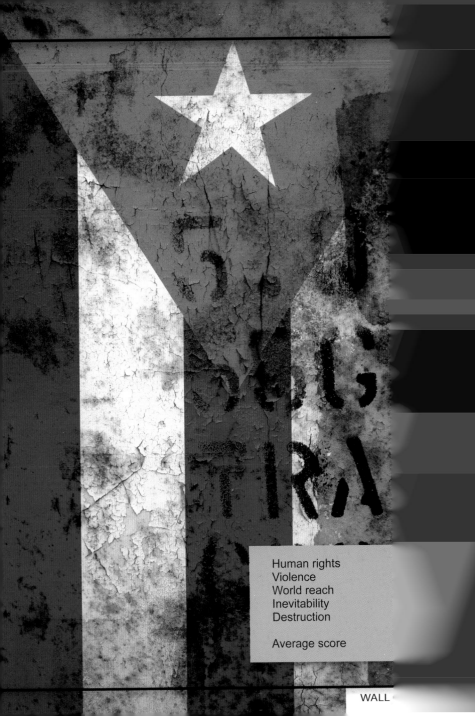

Human rights
Violence
World reach
Inevitability
Destruction

Average score

WALL

Human rights	0/10
Violence	0/10
World reach	8/10
Inevitability	7/10
Destruction	7.5/10
Average score	4.5/10

Kimberly Murray: Part of the problem is our dependence on the goods mining gives us: steel for building, luxuries like gold and silver, metal for the coins of our currency, and all the metal wiring we use for electricity and other purposes. We need to find alternatives to these non-renewable resources!

For centuries, humans have been exploiting the earth for minerals for all kinds of purposes. Mining for coal, gold, iron, and other metal-producing ore is the way to economic development for many towns and countries, and, not surprisingly, it has been at the center of wars, mass murders, racial injustices, and environmental disasters. It can lead to erosion, sinkholes, loss of biodiversity and soil, and groundwater contamination. It also often causes serious health issues for miners and their communities.

Mining is invasive, and the pollution it causes is mindboggling. Mines destroy forests, hillsides, and natural environments that wildlife depend on. Some kinds of mines result in sulfuric acid being dumped into local water, air, and land. In Canada, it is estimated that

Opposite page: Water pollution from copper mining.
Left: Pouring waste directly into a river.
Below: Open pit mine with contaminated water.

mining generates over a billion tonnes of waste annually, about twenty times the amount of waste produced by an average-sized city. A gold wedding ring causes between six and twenty tonnes of waste rock and tailings to be produced. Water is an integral part of the mining process: clean water goes in and contaminated water comes out. It is used to wash the extracted ore and is used in the milling and refining processes and to clean the waste material from the mill.

Mining is also a major contributor to climate change; its ecological footprint is devastating. For example, one tonne of aluminum produces four tonnes of greenhouse gases. Coal is the largest contributor to the human-made increase of CO_2 in the atmosphere.

Mining also takes a toll on the miners who work in the industry. Deaths occur from mining accidents, such as cave-ins or gas leaks and poisoning. Pneumoconiosis (CWP), also known as black lung disease, is caused by continued exposure to coal dust and is a near inevitability for coal miners.

Patrick Bonneville: It is tragic that in a democracy, a political group would resort to terrorism to make themselves heard. They should muster the courage to find other means to get their message across.

The beautiful Western Pyrenees are home to a special region, the Basque Country, which crosses the border between France and Spain. It has a unique flavor, culture, and language. It is also home to a strong nationalist movement, which has sought autonomy for the Basque people from Spain.

One particular organization in this movement took up arms and terrorist strategies in their quest for independence. Since 1968, the *Euskadi Ta Askatasuna,* better known as ETA, has terrorized Spain and the South of France with violence, including assassinations and bombings. This small group numbers fewer than a thousand individuals, many of whom are now in prison. Politically, the ETA does not represent the views of the majority of the Basque population.

The Marxist-Leninist organization was founded by young nationalists in Spain during Francisco Franco's dictatorship. After Franco's death in 1975, Spain turned to democracy and granted the Greater Basque Country a certain level of autonomy. During the transition period, ETA was active and began to commit terrorist acts that would eventually take hundreds of lives. Their bombings and shootings have been especially targeted at police and military officials, journalists, and politicians. They have not spared civilians, although they often announce an impending bombing with an anonymous call to newspapers. This gives them the exposure they desire and allows them to reduce "collateral damage."

"We will eradicate all the bases of ETA one by one. We won't let France become the support base of terrorists and assassins."
—French President Nicolas Sarkozy

Human rights	6.5/10
Violence	6/10
World reach	2/10
Inevitability	5/10
Destruction	3/10
Average score	4.5/10

Right: Guardia Civil barracks in the northern city of Burgos, Spain, after the July 2009 bombing.

Patrick Bonneville: Faced with the poverty problems of developing nations, including high infant mortality, malnourishment, and HIV/AIDS, how can the Vatican continue to condemn birth control and be against condoms? It is the cause of much suffering in the world.

Above: According to Pope Benedict XVI, chastity and fidelity in marriage, not condoms, are the ways to combat HIV and AIDS.

The Roman Catholic Church is officially opposed to the idea of contraception and disapproves of sexual acts outside marriage. They are considered mortal sins. The only acceptable form of birth control is abstinence. In 1968, Pope Paul VI approved of Natural Family Planning (NFP), which involves periodical abstinence, but he was quick to condemn non-natural contraception.

Of all the world's major religions, the Roman Catholic church is unique in its opposition to birth control. This, despite a current world population of well over 6.5 billion, according to the World Bank. Family planning and contraception are the best methods for controlling our numbers.

The Vatican has also been submergered by yet another scandal. During the last two decades of the twentieth century, reports of pedophilia in the Catholic Church began to make headlines in several countries around the world. Adult survivors—some women, but mostly men—stepped forward to testify about how they had been drawn into or subjected to sexual activities with priests when they were children.

The victims, some of them poor, some of them privileged, reported that their lives had been ruined by the abuse. Indeed, in many cases, the testimony was met by the Church with denial or at least with few real consequences for the priests involved. In many cases, it is alleged, the Church simply transferred the perpetrator to another region, where his behavior could continue, rather than reporting the matter to the proper authorities.

"The traditional teaching of the church has proven to be the only failsafe way to prevent the spread of HIV/AIDS."
—Pope Benedict XVI, 2005

Human rights	2/10
Violence	0/10
World reach	10/10
Inevitability	10/10
Destruction	0/10
Average score	4.4/10

US DEPARTMENT OF JUSTICE

Patrick Bonneville: "In bankers and brokers we trust." A certain Bernard Madoff might have changed that concept.

Left: The most notorious operator of large-scale fraud in recent history, stockbroker and financial adviser Bernard Madoff.

There are many types of financial fraud prevalent today, many of them targeted at wealthy people seeking to increase their wealth or at hopeful people hoping to acquire some. A Ponzi scheme is a deceptive investment ploy that eventually leaves its participants stripped of their capital investment. A Ponzi scheme organizer deals directly with individual investors, promising them huge payouts. He or she initially pays investors returns from their own money or with money paid by other investors; there is seldom actually any real profit-generating investment. Based on insider information, Ponzi schemes generally attract well-to-do investors. This style of fraud is named for Charles Ponzi, who, in the 1920s, became notorious for using the method to build his personal fortune.

Multi-level pyramid schemes also offer promised returns, but they function differently. Pyramid scheme organizers do not deal with each investor; instead, participants have contact with the person who recruited them. New recruits must recruit other investors in order to see a trickle-up return; payouts come from the next new investor. While these may initially seem like no-risk investments, as the pyramid grows, more and more investments are needed to feed the first investors and the system is bound to collapse.

In one of the largest and most notorious Ponzi schemes known, American investment advisor Bernard L. Madoff fleeced his investors of billions of dollars. In 2009, Madoff confessed to organizing a Ponzi scheme under the name Bernard L. Madoff Investment Securities LLC. He had begun operating in 1960. On June 29, 2009, he was sentenced to 150 years in prison and was obliged to make $170 billion in restitution for his role in what is called the largest investor fraud ever committed by an individual. At least 13,500 different accounts had been listed as bankrupt as a direct result of investing with Madoff, including banks, hedge funds, universities, charities, and several wealthy individuals. One of his clients was the Elie Wiesel Foundation for Humanity—which, incidentally, lost $15.2 million.

Human rights	2/10
Violence	0/10
World reach	10/10
Inevitability	10/10
Destruction	0/10
Average score	4.4/10

Patrick Bonneville: Human negligence has cost the lives of many innocent people. The Vajont Dam disaster in Italy is a good example of this: despite warnings to the state from engineers, an overflow in 1959 proved deadly.

Dams are designed to either contain or control the flow of water, usually for the production of hydroelectricity. They often disrupt the natural environment and cause enormous ecological damage. UNESCO has called the Vajont Dam accident one of the five worst man-made disasters caused by the "failure of engineers and geologists."

In 1959, in the valley of the Vajont River, just 100 kilometers north of Venice, Italy, the construction of a hydroelectric dam was completed. Four years later, an enormous and rapid landslide splashed into the dam's reservoir, causing a 250-meter-high wave (820 feet) to "top over" the dam. The wave flooded the valley below, wiping out several villages and killing 2,000 people.

Experts had reported problems with the dam's placement from its earliest phases of construction. Some efforts to correct flaws were undertaken and in 1962 the dam's basin was filled to capacity. Complaints from citizens of the villages below about increased ground movements fell on deaf ears. On September 15, the entire side of Mount Toc, which bordered the reservoir, shifted downward by 22 centimeters (about 8.6 inches). Eleven days later, the company decided to slowly reduce the amount of water in the basin. It was too little, too late, though: in early October, the mountain dropped by almost a meter, and instead of warning the public or issuing an evacuation order, authorities ignored the phenomenon.

On October 9, 1963, at approximately 10:35 p.m., disaster hit. Heavy rains combined with the slow release of water from the basin triggered 260 million cubic meters of forest, earth, and rock to slide down the side of Mount Toc and into the dam's reservoir. The landslide, traveling at about 110 kilometers an hour (68 mph), caused a gigantic wave to splash over the dam and flood the Piave valley. It is estimated that about 350 families were completely wiped out, the few surviving children left orphans.

Above: Memorial in honor of the vicitims.

Human rights	0/10
Violence	0/10
World reach	1.5/10
Inevitability	10/10
Destruction	10/10
Average score	4.3/10

Ritual servitude is an traditional African religious practice popular in Ghana, Togo, and Benin. It most often involves young female virgins, called Trokosi. Generally under the age of ten, and sometimes as young as three, these girls are given to religious idol shrines to serve as "wives of the gods" as atonement for misdeeds on the part of their families. Usually the misdeed being atoned for is one committed by a female family member. Girls are also given in payment for a service offered by a god. If a priest or elder of the shrine has helped a family with healing or conceiving, for example, a daughter might be given in servitude.

Right: Girls before their rescue from Trokosi slavery.

The Trokosi girls effectively become shrine slaves, serving the priests and elders of the village. They are placed into servitude without their consent, they are not paid, they receive no education, and they suffer harsh punishments. Many of them have revealed to humanitarian organizations that they were sexually abused.

Although defenders of ritual servitude object to it being called slavery—the young girls choose their servitude and are respected in their communities, they say—human rights organizations believe the girls are, effectively, modern-day slaves. They become the property of the shrine they serve. In some countries the practice continues despite the threat of imprisonment, and some families place as many as three or four of their daughters in servitude.

Non-governmental organizations have been very active in fighting the practice. Since the 1990s, many shrines have been closed and some laws have been passed to ban ritual servitude.

"The most disturbing detail is that although the trokosi system, alongside all traditional and cultural practices that violate the constitution of Ghana, was banned in 1998 the practice is still very much alive."
—Nana Sekyiamah, African Women's Development Fund, July 2008

Human rights	9/10
Violence	0/10
World reach	1/10
Inevitability	10/10
Destruction	0/10
Average score	4.0/10

Patrick Bonneville: Trawling the ocean floor leads to overfishing but worst of all, it stirs up everything lying there, damaging this whole ecosystem. Unfortunately, this kind of fishing is easily hidden from view. As Kim Murray says, "You have to ask yourself: is that plate of orange roughy worth destroying our environment?"

Above: A modern trawler in Denmark.

Bottom trawling, or dragging fish nets along the ocean floor, razes the ecosystem that thrives there. A commercial trawler can, in just a few short months, destroy what took nature thousands of years to create. Studies show that annually, an area twice the size of the United States is destroyed because of bottom trawling. These disastrous effects have led the United Nations to call for a ban on high seas bottom trawling.

Bottom trawlers' nets are rigged with steel plates and heavy rollers. Their by-catch includes thousands of tons of coral which is tossed back into the ocean, dead or dying. Fragile coral reefs are an important part of the ocean ecosystem: they provide shelter, food, oxygen, and clean the water. Their destruction means certain death for thousands of sea sponges, fish, crustaceans, plankton, algae, and other species who rely on coral. Once destroyed, a reef can take centuries to recover; some never do. In 1997, off the coast of Australia, commercial fishermen reeled in about 4,000 tons of orange roughy, a deep-sea fish. Their catch also included 10,000 tons of destroyed coral.

Bottom trawling also stirs up sediment. On flat ocean surfaces, the sediment can easily block sunlight from reaching lower levels of the ocean. This has a direct impact on aquatic plants, and of course if there are fewer ocean plants, there is less food and shelter for fish. Other innocent victims of bottom trawling include dolphins, sharks, sea turtles, and even sea birds. An estimated 22-42 million tons of unintended catch is thrown back yearly.

"Ancient forests in danger ... deep under the ocean. Biologists estimate that somewhere between 500,000 and 5,000,000 marine species have yet to be discovered. But many of these species are in serious danger from the world's most destructive fishing practice—bottom trawling."
—Greenpeace

Human rights	0/10
Violence	0/10
World reach	7/10
Inevitability	8/10
Destruction	5/10
Average score	4.0/10

Patrick Bonneville: Why is New Orleans on our Wall of Shame? For two reasons: city planners didn't do their jobs in developing neighborhoods that were sustainable in light of the city's vulnerability to flooding. Second, after 2005's Hurricane Katrina, the response of the American federal government, the most powerful nation in the world, was inexcusably insufficient. Nevertheless, beautiful New Orleans and its people still have a very special place in the hearts of Americans and visitors from all over the world.

As one of the oldest cities in the United States, New Orleans has a rich and unique history. Its multicultural streets are filled with stories, music, and laughter. New Orleans has color and pizzazz.

The part of the city that lacks sparkle, however, is its infrastructure. City engineer A. Baldwin Wood was hired by the Sewerage & Water Board of New Orleans in 1899 to design a system that would improve drainage from the flood-prone city. They were eager to extend urban development to the low-lying areas around the port. Wood invented the "flapgate" and other hydraulic devices that would allow for the expansion of the city to terrain below sea level.

The folly of this approach to development was evident in 1965, when Hurricane Betsy ripped through the area, killing dozens in the low-lying region and leaving upper New Orleans unscathed. Thirty years later, in 1995, severe rains flooded the region, due in part to weaknesses in the pumping system.

But the worst disaster to hit this part of town was Hurricane Katrina, on August 29, 2005. Katrina hit land at 225 kilometers an hour (140 mph). At least 1,033 people were killed. More than a million residents of the Gulf Coast were displaced. Four days after the disaster, New Orleans Mayor Ray Nagin noted the absence of federal aid as his flooded city lost more and more victims while waiting for government assistance.

Human rights	0/10
Violence	0/10
World reach	1/10
Inevitability	10/10
Destruction	9/10
Average score	4.0/10

Left: New Orleans after the passage of the hurricane.
Right: After Hurricane Katrina, most roads in the region were damaged or flooded.

"Following the oil and its impacts over the past 20 years has changed our understanding of the long-term damage from an oil spill. . . Exxon Valdez oil persists in the environment and, in places, is nearly as toxic as it was the first few weeks after the spill."
- Exxon Valdez Oil Spill Trustee Council

Human rights	0/10
Violence	0/10
World reach	2/10
Inevitability	9/10
Destruction	9/10
Average score	4.0/10

Patrick Bonneville: Petroleum spills cause much destruction. Beaches along this remote Alaskan coastline were black with oil, and coastal birds and other creatures of the sea were covered with the stuff. This is one more reason to turn toward cleaner sources of energy.

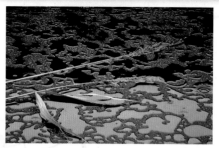

Left: Exxon Valdes is history's worst oil spill.
Above: Oil floats on top of water, affecting fauna, flora and the whole ecosytem of a region.

On March 23, 1989, the oil tanker ship Exxon Valdez left the Valdez oil terminal in Alaska for Long Beach, California. About twenty-four hours later, the ship's captain obtained permission to travel through the inbound lane, as icebergs were too numerous to navigate. At four minutes past midnight, on March 24, the Exxon Valdez hit the Bligh Reef in Prince William Sound and began to leak oil. A storm surging through the region pushed huge quantities of the oil onto the shore. According to official reports, the ship was carrying 53.1 million U.S. gallons, of which 10.8 million spilled into Prince William Sound. Some environmental organizations claim that this is an underestimation. The oil eventually covered some 1,300 square miles (3,400 km²) of ocean.

As a first cleanup action, a dispersant was applied directly to the spill. Not enough waves were present to effectively mix the solution with the oil, however. Next, explosions were detonated to burn off the oil. This had limited success, but poor weather prohibited further efforts. Extensive manual cleanup efforts continued with help from about 11,000 Alaskan residents. It was difficult, and in some areas the task was next to impossible.

It has now been over twenty years since the spill. Plankton and microbial organisms reduce the oil contamination by less than 4 percent annually, but experts say it will be decades before the Sound is returned to its pre-spill state. A study conducted by the National Oceanic and Atmospheric Administration in 2007 reported more than 26,000 U.S. gallons of oil remained along the contaminated shoreline. The captain of the Exxon Valdez was found guilty of negligent discharge of oil and was fined $50,000 and sentenced to 1,000 hours of community service. Exxon estimates it spent $2.1 billion over the following four summers to clean up after the tanker spill. Commercial fishermen and other Alaskan residents sued Exxon for damages after the spill, and in 2008, the company was obligated to pay out 75 percent of a $507.5 million damages claim.

Although this spill is not the biggest in volume on record, it is the worst spill in history in terms of environmental damage.

In August 2006, poachers destroyed at least 100 African elephants in eight days in the vicinity of Zakouma National Park in south-eastern Chad. The poverty of the Chadian people and the high value of illegal elephant ivory on the international black market have meant an ugly history of killing these majestic creatures. The animals were brutally murdered, their faces mutilated from the effort to retrieve their ivory tusks. Their bodies were left to rot. Zakouma National Park was created in 1963 to protect elephants within its borders. When elephants wander outside the protective zone to forage, however, they are vulnerable to horse-mounted poachers armed with Kalashnikov rifles. The Chadian elephant population decreased from 300,000 in 1970 to approximately 10,000 in 2006.

Above: Director of Zakouma National Park, Luis Arranz, with a local ranger.

Although hunting is illegal and a ban on the sale of ivory has been in place since 1989, its trade on the black-market is actually increasing. Between 1996 and 2002, reports say that forty-five tons of ivory was seized by Chinese authorities. The demand for ivory is so strong that the overall African elephant population has dropped from 1.3 million to about 600,000 in the span of twenty years. Savannah elephants have been the hardest hit, since their tusks are the biggest. In 1990, the Convention on International Trade in Endangered Species (CITES) banned the sale of ivory. This ban helped to stabilize elephant populations, however some countries have benefited from exempt status: Zimbabwe, Botswana, and Namibia can sell ivory to Japan.

More recently, Kenyan poachers have begun using poisoned arrows to kill elephants. Poisoned arrows make it difficult for officials to track down the poacher because there are no bullet traces to follow. Plus, the poison used is very effective, easy to come by (it grows naturally in Kenya), and creates far less attention than shooting. Kenyan officials feel the increase in recent elephant killings in that country is a direct response to the lifted ban on the trade of ivory with Japan.

Human rights	0/10
Violence	1/10
World reach	1/10
Inevitability	10/10
Destruction	8/10
Average score	4.0/10

Some uprisings are necessary for social change. They are good events for humanity. Others, such as hooliganism, police riots, prison riots or even student riots often lead to unecessary use of force, vandalism and death of innocent bystanders.

"Some died of suffocation but the majority seem to have been killed by being crushed."
—*Policeman Daniel Twum, explaining the death of 125 people in a stampede at a football stadium in Ghana*

"I can see in your eyes, I can see in your faces, I can see you cry. But what I want to say, there's no reason to cry. Do not, in the name of peace, go in the streets and riot."
—*Football player George Weah*

Rioting is civil disorder. It is the act of sudden and intense violence, vandalism or other crimes (such as police bashing). Riots can occur from a perceived situation. For example, historically we know of rioting among poor people against their governments. We saw the French Revolution grow from citizens taking to the streets (Bastille Day). In cases of grievances with authority, riots will focus on destruction of those authority icons, such as government buildings, churches, public squares, or statues of past heros.

In states where riots are more frequent, the rioters have grown sophisticated. They can predict police tactics and prepare in advance for these tactics. With the onset of the internet, information on how to riot can be shared.

Controlling and dealing with riots can be difficult. Police need to use force – but just how much before someone claims police brutality? And each country's threshold for such justice is different. Where it might be common place to use tear gas or riot shotguns in some nations, the idea of that in others is horrendous!

Human rights	1/10
Violence	3/10
World reach	7/10
Inevitability	7/10
Destruction	2/10
Average score	4.0/10

Patrick Bonneville: I used to be an advertising consultant for major brands. I know that advertising works—otherwise, it wouldn't exist. If informed adults are so easily influenced by advertising, imagine the effects on children. They see it. They like it. They want it. Fortunately, in many countries advertising directed at children is banned or restricted. In others, such as the United States, advertising is an "open tap."

Children have amazing pull in the world of commerce. It is estimated that in the year 2000, children under thirteen years of age were responsible for the spending of over $600 billion in the United States alone. The American advertising industry is smart—they've learned how to manipulate that market and create advertising specifically for children.

The average American child sees hundreds of advertisements a day, in logos, jingles, TV and radio commercials, branded toys and clothes and lunchboxes, plus posters and billboards. In one year, he or she has watched 40,000 television commercials. While some countries—the UK, Canada, Greece, Denmark, Belgium, Sweden, and Norway—have restricted children's advertising, in the United States, the trend of bombarding children with cleverly placed ads is only increasing.

The marketing manipulations are cunning. Savvy companies hire child psychologists to design pitches that will appeal to the sensibilities and desires of a particular age group. Indeed, the best advertisers create a "need" in the child for the product they are promoting. Some magazine ads are disguised as comic stories or as letters to experts. Other marketing ploys imply that the child is a "loser" if he or she does not have the latest electronic gizmo or item of clothing.

Adding to the complexity of the problem is the advertising directed at adults that children are exposed to in their daily lives. Children see that junk food is delicious and affordable, and yet they also see that the diet and exercise industries are in full bloom. They see female sexuality used to sell food, clothes, cars, and alcohol.

Above: TV is a very efficient way to reach a young audience.

Human rights	2/10
Violence	0/10
World reach	9/10
Inevitability	9/10
Destruction	0/10
Average score	4.0/10

Patrick Bonneville: Dolphins are some of the most lovable creatures on earth. When we visit the world's aquariums, theme parks and aquatic pens, however, we need to be aware of animal welfare issues as we watch the dolphins play and perform.

It's hard not to love a dolphin: they look as though they are always smiling! And yet they are surely not smiling in their dolphinariums. Kept in pools or pens in the ocean for research, education, or public entertainment, the captive dolphins that serve us have been shown to suffer from stress, and can be aggressive.

The first recorded dolphin show was in St. Augustine, Florida in 1938. Dolphins had been herded into the Marine Studios dolphinarium, where people paid to see them perform tricks. Today, dolphinariums are exempt from United States' 1972 Marine Mammal Protection Act, under the assertion that the captivity of dolphins promotes their conservation and protection. There are, nevertheless, strict regulations regarding the size of the pools, how the dolphins can be acquired—mainly through captive birthing rather than ocean trapping—how they can be treated, and the types of entertainment they can be forced to do.

Today, there are no dolphinariums in the UK or Australia. Japan, however, is home to fifty dolphinariums. SaveJapanDolphins.org suggests that some members of the international aquarium and zoo industry are strongly connected to the Japanese commercial dolphin fishery: they are ready to pay top dollar for specimens deemed suitable for commercial exploitation in dolphin shows and captive dolphin swim programs. Live dolphins captured in a Taiji dolphin drive hunt recently sold for $154,000 per mammal. Several of the hundreds of captive dolphins in Japan's dolphinariums were obtained through the dolphin drive hunts, yet the dolphinariums do nothing to educate the public about the hunt.

"Held in a confined space and subjected to forced interaction with humans, aggressive behaviour (by the dolphins) can have serious consequences."
—Whale and Dolphin Conservation Society

ight: Taiji dolphin hunting drive in Japan.

Human rights	0/10
Violence	2/10
World reach	8/10
Inevitability	9/10
Destruction	1/10
Average score	4.0/10

PHOTO CREDITS

The following abbreviations are used:

b = background
l = left
r = right
u = upper

4	Leo21cn/Dreamstime.com
6	Aron Brand/Shutterstock
10	Serdar Tibet/Dreamstime.com
12	Satori13/Dreamstime.com
14	Ron Chapple Studios/Dreamstime.com
16	Ken Brown/Dreamstime.com
16 b	U.S. National Archives
17	Tim De Boeck/Dreamstime.com
18	Denis Dryashkin/Dreamstime.com
19	Robert Lindeboom/Dreamstime.com
19 b	Geoffrey Kuchera/Shutterstock
20 b	Matt Trommer/Shutterstock
20	Wangxiaoting for Shanghai Journal
21	U.S. National Archives and Records
22 b	Loic Giraud/Shutterstock
24	Bliznetsov/Shutterstock
26	Justin Paget/Shutterstock
26	Photobunny/Shutterstock
27	Russ Du parcq/Shutterstock
28	Alen/Shutterstock
29	Konstantynov/Shutterstock
30	ILO
31 b	Gerald Bernard/Dreamstime.com
32	Eugene Ivanov/Shutterstock
34	Yuri4u80/Dreamstime.com
34 b	Kirill Derjugin/Dreamstime.com
35	Vincent de Groot
36 b	Alexeyzel/Dreamstime.com
37	Oleksii Sergieiev/Dreamstime.com
39	Penny Mathews/Dreamstime.com
40	Micropix/Dreamstime.com
41	Unknown
41	Unknown
41 b	Penny Mathews/Dreamstime.com
42 b	Penny Mathews/Dreamstime.com
43	Bernardo Ertl/Dreamstime.com
44	Sebastian Kaulitzki/Dreamstime.com
46 b	Neale Cousland/dreamstime.com
46	U.S. National Archives
47 b	Stocklight/Shutterstock
47	Rolffimages/Dreamstime.com
48	Tara Flake/Shutterstock
48 b	Bill Ragan/Shutterstock
49	Jeremyrichards/Dreamstime.com
50	USIA/DOD
51	Michael Zysman/Shutterstock
51 b	Mcpics/Dreamstime.com
52	UN Photo/John Isaac
53 b	Davinci/Dreamstime.com
53	UN Photo/John Isaac
54 b	Ruslan Gilmanshin/Dreamstime.com
56	Connors Bros/Shutterstock
56 b	Ruslan Gilmanshin/Dreamstime.com
57	Philip Date/Shutterstock
58	Shariff Che' Lah/Dreamstime.com
60	Matt Fowler/Dreamstime.com
62 b	David Snyder/Dreamstime.com
63	UN Photo/Tim McKulka
64 b	Pontus Edenberg/Dreamstime.com
65	U.S. Navy/Jesse B. Awalt
66	Anthony Correia/Shutterstock
68 b	Anthony Correia/Shutterstock
69	kentannenbaum.com/dreamstime.com
70	Svlumagraphica/Dreamstime.com
71 b	Cheryl Casey/Dreamstime.com
72	Konstantin32/Dreamstime.com
74 b	Dariush M./Shutterstock
75	Lforquer/Dreamstime.com
76	Ramzi Hachicho/Shutterstock
76 b	Robert Ad. Hillman/Dreamstime.com
77	UN Photo/X
78 b	Cpenler/Dreamstime.com
79	Rick Lippiett/Dreamstime.com
80 b	Photoeuphoria/Dreamstime.com
82	Eldin/Shutterstock

84	UN Photo/R LeMoyne	111	U.S. Army
85 b	Orhan/Shutterstock	112	S.Al Fattah Khan/Dreamstime.com
85 r	Adam Jones Adam	114	Ivan Stanic/Dreamstime.com
85 l	Hedwig Klawuttke	114 b	Madartists/Dreamstime.com
86 b	Eldin/Shutterstock	116	Brian Akerson/Dreamstime.com
86	U.S. Air Force/Brian Schlumbohm	116 b	Ragsac19/Dreamstime.com
86	UN Photo/R LeMoyne	117	Gina Smith/Dreamstime.com
87	UN Photo/U Meissner	118 b	Lizette Potgieter/Shutterstock
88	Wrangler/Shutterstock	119	Sebastian Knight/Shutterstock
90	Natalia Medvedeva	120	Stephen Mulcahey/Shutterstock
90 b	Aniram/Dreamstime.com	121 b	Steve Mann/Dreamstime.com
91	Olira/Dreamstime.com	122 b	Ruslan Gilmanshin/Dreamstime.com
92	Digigerrit/Dreamstime.com	122	Mark Rhomberg/ETAN
93	Mikael Damkier/Shutterstock	123	UN Photo/Martine Perret
94 b	GERSHBERG Yuri/Shutterstock	124 b	Ldambies/Dreamstime.com
94 r	Filmcrew/Dreamstime.com	124	PH3 Henry Cleveland, USN
94 l	Natalia Bratslavsky/Dreamstime.com	125	Project Get Out and Walk
95	Terry Poche/Dreamstime.com	126 b	Michael Schmeling/Dreamstime.com
96	Olga Besnard/Shutterstock	126	Aleksandr S. Khachunts/Shutterstock
97	GERSHBERG Yuri/Shutterstock	128	Liubomir Turcanu/Dreamstime.com
97 b	Mikhail Levit/Shutterstock	129	Sayeed Janbozorgi
98	Roger Mcclean3Dreamstime.com	129 b	Andreas Gradin/Dreamstime.com
99 l	United Nations	130	Gilmanshin/Shutterstock
99 b	UN Photo/A Tannenbaum	131	Kots/Shutterstock
99 r	United Nations	132 b	AridOcean/Shutterstock
101 l	United Nations	133	UN Photo/Milton Grant
101 r	UN Photo/P Sudhakaran	134 b	UN Photo/Eric Kanalstein
102	UN Photo/Martine Perret	136 b	Kacpura/Dreamstime.com
103	UN Photo	137	UN Photo/Eric Kanalstein
103 b	Dreamstock73/Dreamstime.com	138	David Blumenkrantz
104	UN Photo	139 b	Ruslan Gilmanshin/Dreamstime.com
104 b	Tomas Marek/Dreamstime.com	140 b	Antloft/Shutterstock
105	UN Photo	141	Alex Hessler/dreamstime.com
106	US Army	142 b	Ruslan Gilmanshin/Dreamstime.com
108	Ragesoss	143	Josef Muellek/Dreamstime.com
109 b	U.S. Army	144	Jennifer Russell/Dreamstime.com
109 l	U.S. Army/Tierney Nowland	146 b	Jennifer Russell/Dreamstime.com
109	U.S. Army	147	World Economic Forum/Monika Flueckiger
110	U.S. Army	148	Shutterstock
111 b	Miroslav Ferkuniak/Dreamstime.com	150	Photawa/Dreamstime.com
111	U.S. Army	152	Unknown

PHOTO CREDITS

"As long as people believe in absurdities they will continue to commit atrocities."
—*Voltaire*